THE ART OF THE MEMOIR

Telling Personal Stories with Universal Appeal

Michael Edgar Lawrence

S.D.N Publishing

Copyright © 2023 S.D.N Publishing

All rights reserved

The characters and events portrayed in this book are fictitious. Any similarity to real persons, living or dead, is coincidental and not intended by the author.

No part of this book may be reproduced, or stored in a retrieval system, or transmitted in any form or by any means, electronic, mechanical, photocopying, recording, or otherwise, without express written permission of the publisher.

ISBN: 9798870604725

CONTENTS

Title Page
Copyright
General Disclaimer — 1
Part I: Introducing Memoirs & Memoir Writing — 3
Understanding the Memoir Genre Defining memoir and its place in literature — 7
The Roots of a Memoir: Finding Your Story Techniques for identifying the core story of your memoir — 10
The Power of Memory: Recalling and Recording — 15
Honing Your Narrative Voice — 18
Part II: Brain to Paper – Structuring, Development and Overcoming Obstacles — 21
The Ethics of Memoir Writing — 25
Overcoming Writer's Block — 28
Writing with Honesty and Vulnerability — 31
Crafting Compelling Openings — 34
Developing Characters in Memoirs — 37
Part III: Setting, Narrative, Description, Dialogue & Pacing — 40
Balancing Narrative and Reflection — 43
The Art of Descriptive Writing — 46
Dialogue in Memoirs — 49

Pacing Your Story	52
Part IV: Themes, Research, Sensitivity, Ethics & Humor	55
Research and Fact-Checking in Memoirs	58
Addressing Sensitive Topics	61
The Role of Humor in Memoirs	64
Writing About Others Ethically	66
Part V: Editing, Amending & Revising & Overcoming Problems	68
Overcoming Self-Doubt and Criticism	71
Finding Inspiration and Staying Motivated	74
Part VI: Elevating Your Content & Key Considerations	77
Crafting a Satisfying Conclusion	80
Legal Considerations in Memoir Writing	82
Part VII: The Personal Impact of Memoir Writing	84
Memoir Writing as a Legacy	87
Part VIII: Mastering Advanced Writing Techniques	89
Mastering Non-Linear Narratives	93
The Use of Symbolism and Metaphor	96
Part IX: Personal and Cultural Influences	99
The Intersection of Memoir and Cultural Commentary	103
Crafting a Unique Authorial Presence	106
Part X: More Advanced Techniques and Reflections	109
The Blending of Genres in Memoirs	113
The Role of Introspection and Self-Analysis	116
Unconventional Formats and Structures	119
The Art of Subtext in Memoirs	123
Advanced Techniques in Descriptive Writing	126
Part XI: Adding Greater Depth to your Memoir	129

Psychological Insights in Character Development	133
The Use of Literary Devices in Memoirs	136
Part XII: The Future, Ethics and Philosophy and Purpose	139
Ethical Dilemmas in Memoir Writing	143
The Intersection of Memoir and Philosophy	146
Part XIII: Even Deeper – Layers that Enhance Emotion	149
The Challenge of Writing About Happiness	153
The Role of Research in Deepening Your Memoir	156
Addressing Global Issues Through Personal Stories	160
The Use of Irony and Paradox in Memoirs	164
Writing About Love and Relationships	168
Part XIV: Responsibilities, Endings and Evolution	172
Advanced Techniques in Crafting Memoir Endings	176
Blurring the Lines Between Fact and Fiction	180
The Evolution of the Memoir Genre	184
The Memoirist as a Cultural Storyteller	188
Embracing Your Journey as a Memoirist	192
THE END	197

GENERAL DISCLAIMER

This book is intended to provide informative and educational material on the subject matter covered. The author(s), publisher, and any affiliated parties make no representations or warranties with respect to the accuracy, applicability, completeness, or suitability of the contents herein and specifically disclaim any implied warranties of merchantability or fitness for a particular purpose.

The information contained in this book is for general information purposes only and is not intended to serve as legal, medical, financial, or any other form of professional advice. Readers should consult with appropriate professionals before making any decisions based on the information provided. Neither the author(s) nor the publisher shall be held responsible or liable for any loss, damage, injury, claim, or otherwise, whether direct or indirect, consequential, or incidental, that may occur as a result of applying or misinterpreting the information in this book.

This book may contain references to third-party websites, products, or services. Such references do not constitute an endorsement or recommendation, and the author(s) and publisher are not responsible for any outcomes related to these third-party references.

In no event shall the author(s), publisher, or any affiliated parties be liable for any direct, indirect, punitive, special, incidental, or other consequential damages arising directly or indirectly from any use of this material, which is provided "as is," and without warranties of any kind, express or implied.

By reading this book, you acknowledge and agree that you assume all risks and responsibilities concerning the applicability and consequences of the information provided. You also agree to indemnify, defend, and hold harmless the author(s), publisher, and any affiliated parties from any and all liabilities, claims, demands, actions, and causes of action whatsoever, whether or not foreseeable, that may arise from using or misusing the information contained in this book.

Although every effort has been made to ensure the accuracy of the information in this book as of the date of publication, the landscape of the subject matter covered is continuously evolving. Therefore, the author(s) and publisher expressly disclaim responsibility for any errors or omissions and reserve the right to update, alter, or revise the content without prior notice.

By continuing to read this book, you agree to be bound by the terms and conditions stated in this disclaimer. If you do not agree with these terms, it is your responsibility to discontinue use of this book immediately.

PART I: INTRODUCING MEMOIRS & MEMOIR WRITING

Welcome to Memoir Writing An engaging introduction to the world of memoir writing.

Memoir writing is an intricate and intimate journey, where personal narratives intersect with universal truths. This art form, deeply rooted in the writer's life experiences, offers a unique perspective that resonates with a broad audience, transcending the individual's story to touch upon common human experiences. The essence of memoir writing lies in the authentic portrayal of one's life, complete with its triumphs, tribulations, and the valuable lessons learned along the way.

Authentic Storytelling

Memoirs stand out in their requirement for authenticity and vulnerability. This genre demands a deep dive into personal experiences, some of which may be challenging or uncomfortable to revisit. The authenticity in memoir writing is not just about factual accuracy; it's about emotional truth. When writers candidly share their feelings, thoughts, and reflections, they create a powerful connection with the reader. This honesty is what transforms a personal anecdote into a universal story.

The Universal in the Personal

In memoir writing, the personal becomes universal. It's about finding those threads of human experience that are relatable to others. The writer's specific experiences, while unique, often evoke shared emotions and situations familiar to the reader. It's not the exact events that matter most but the emotions and insights that emerge from them. The skill of the memoirist lies in weaving these personal tales in a way that they strike a chord with the broader audience, offering a mirror to their own lives.

Reflection and Insight

Memoirs go beyond mere recollection of events; they delve into the realm of reflection and insight. The genre calls for introspection, allowing the writer to explore the deeper meanings and implications of their experiences. This reflective aspect distinguishes memoirs from simple autobiographies. It's not just about what happened, but about what was learned, how it changed the writer, and what it can teach others.

The Art of Crafting a Memoir

The process of creating a memoir involves several key components:

- **Narrative Structure**: Memoirs often adopt a non-linear narrative, focusing on specific themes or experiences rather than a chronological recounting of the writer's entire life. This approach allows for a more thematic and engaging storytelling experience.
- **Character Portrayal**: In memoirs, real-life characters, including the writer, are portrayed with depth and complexity. The challenge lies in presenting these characters truthfully yet empathetically, showing their multifaceted natures.
- **Contextual Richness**: The setting, whether it be a physical location or a historical/cultural backdrop, adds richness to the memoir, anchoring the narrative in a specific time and place, thereby enhancing the reader's immersion.
- **Language and Tone**: The choice of language and the tone of the memoir greatly influence its impact. The writer's voice can range from poetic and lyrical to straightforward and conversational, depending on the story and the intended audience.

Memoir writing is a powerful tool for connection and reflection. It's a genre that allows writers to share their personal stories while offering readers a window into experiences that, though specific, echo with universal themes of human life. By turning personal memories into compelling narratives, memoir writers not only preserve their own stories but also contribute to a collective human experience, bridging gaps and fostering understanding across different lives and cultures.

UNDERSTANDING THE MEMOIR GENRE DEFINING MEMOIR AND ITS PLACE IN LITERATURE

Memoir, as a genre, is distinct in the landscape of literature. It occupies a space where personal narratives intermingle with broader literary elements, offering readers insights into individual experiences while connecting them to universal themes. Understanding memoir as a genre involves exploring its definition, its scope, and its place in the literary world.

Defining Memoir

Memoir is often seen as a subset of autobiography, but with a more focused approach. Unlike autobiographies, which typically cover the author's entire life, memoirs concentrate on specific periods or themes within one's life. This focus allows memoirists to delve deeper into particular experiences, emotions, and reflections. The memoir is not just about recounting life events; it's about drawing meaning from them, offering insights and understanding that extend beyond the personal story.

Memoir's Place in Literature

Memoir holds a unique position in literature. It bridges the gap between autobiography and personal essay, combining factual life narratives with introspective and analytical writing. This blend allows memoirs to be both informative and reflective, providing a narrative that is as much about internal landscapes as external events. Memoirs offer a window into the author's world, but they also hold up a mirror to societal and cultural realities, connecting personal stories to larger human experiences.

The Scope of Memoir

The scope of memoir writing is vast and varied. Memoirs can cover a wide range of topics, from childhood memories and personal triumphs to struggles with illness, loss, or identity. The subject matter of a memoir is often deeply personal and can be intensely emotional. However, the best memoirs are those that manage to translate these personal experiences into stories with universal resonance, allowing readers from different backgrounds to find something relatable or insightful within them.

Memoir and Truth

A central aspect of memoir is its relationship with truth. Memoirs are grounded in the truth of the author's experiences, but they are also shaped by the author's perception and memory. This subjective nature of memoir writing means that it is not just a factual recounting of events but an interpretation of those events through the author's lens. The memoirist's task is to navigate this subjective truth with honesty and integrity, creating a narrative that is true to their experience while acknowledging its subjectivity.

Memoir as a genre offers a rich and complex tapestry of storytelling, blending the personal with the universal, the factual with the reflective. It invites readers into the author's world, sharing experiences that are uniquely personal yet resonate with broader themes of human life. In doing so, memoirs contribute to a deeper understanding of the human experience, bridging gaps between different lives and fostering empathy and insight.

THE ROOTS OF A MEMOIR: FINDING YOUR STORY TECHNIQUES FOR IDENTIFYING THE CORE STORY OF YOUR MEMOIR

In the realm of memoir writing, identifying the core story is a crucial step. This process involves introspection and a deep understanding of one's experiences and the significance they hold. The core story of a memoir is not just a sequence of events but a narrative that resonates with emotional truth and personal growth.

Techniques for Identifying the Core Story

1. **Reflective Journaling**: Keeping a journal can be a powerful tool for memoirists. It allows writers to record their thoughts, feelings, and memories, providing a rich source of material to draw upon.

Through journaling, writers can identify recurring themes, significant events, and emotional turning points that could form the basis of their memoir.

2. **Life Mapping**: This technique involves creating a visual representation of one's life. By mapping out key life events, relationships, and experiences, memoirists can gain a clearer understanding of the pivotal moments and themes that define their stories. Life mapping can also help in identifying connections between different events and how they've shaped the writer's life.

3. **Seeking Feedback**: Sometimes, discussing life stories with friends, family, or writing groups can provide new perspectives. Others might point out aspects of one's story that are particularly compelling or unique, which the writer might have overlooked.

4. **Reading Widely**: Engaging with a variety of memoirs can inspire writers and help them understand different ways of structuring a narrative. By exploring how other memoirists have tackled their life stories, writers can gain insights into how to frame their own experiences effectively.

Finding the Emotional Core

The emotional core of a memoir is what connects the writer to the reader. It's the universal element in the story that transcends the specifics of the writer's experiences. Identifying this emotional core involves introspection and honesty. Writers need to ask themselves what emotions their experiences evoke and how these emotions have shaped their understanding of themselves and the world.

The Role of Significant Life Events

Significant life events often serve as anchors in a memoir. These events can be joyous, traumatic, transformative, or a combination of these. The key is not just in narrating these events but in exploring their impact and how they've contributed to the writer's personal growth and understanding. The way these events are woven into the narrative can provide structure and momentum to the memoir.

The Importance of Universal Themes

While memoirs are deeply personal, their appeal often lies in their exploration of universal themes. Themes like love, loss, struggle, resilience, and identity are common in memoir writing because they speak to shared human experiences. Identifying these themes in one's story can help in crafting a narrative that resonates with a wider audience.

Identifying the core story in memoir writing is a process that requires time, introspection, and a willingness to delve into one's past. It's about finding the narrative thread that not only ties the memoir together but also connects the writer's personal experiences to the broader tapestry of human experience. This process is essential in transforming a collection of memories into a cohesive, compelling, and relatable memoir.

Memoir vs. Autobiography: Knowing the Difference

Differentiating between a memoir and an autobiography is crucial for writers embarking on the journey of personal storytelling. Both genres involve the author narrating their life stories, but they differ in scope, focus, and narrative style. Understanding these differences helps writers choose the right format for their story and ensures that their work aligns with the expectations of their readers.

Scope and Focus

The primary difference between a memoir and an autobiography lies in their scope. An autobiography is a comprehensive narrative that covers the author's life from birth to the present, often focusing on the chronology of events. In contrast, a memoir typically concentrates on a specific aspect, theme, or period of the author's life. This focused approach allows memoirs to delve deeper into particular experiences, emotions, and insights, offering a more intimate and reflective narrative.

Narrative Style

The narrative style of memoirs and autobiographies also differs significantly. Autobiographies often adopt a more formal and factual tone, emphasizing the accurate recounting of the author's life events. Memoirs, on the other hand, are usually more narrative and stylistic, employing literary techniques akin to fiction. This style allows memoirists to explore their memories and emotions more creatively, presenting their stories in a way that is not just informative but also evocative and engaging.

Personal vs. Historical Perspective

Autobiographies often serve a dual purpose: they are personal histories as well as documents of the times in which the author lived. As such, they frequently provide insights into historical events and social contexts, offering a broader perspective on the era they cover. Memoirs, while they can also reflect on historical and cultural backgrounds, are primarily introspective, focusing on the author's internal landscape – their emotions, experiences, and personal growth.

Subjectivity and Memory

Both memoirs and autobiographies are subjective, colored by the author's memories and perceptions. However, memoirs embrace this subjectivity more openly, often acknowledging the fallibility of memory and the personal bias in the narration. This acknowledgment allows memoirists to explore their truths in a way that is less about factual accuracy and more about emotional and experiential truth.

Choosing the Right Form

For writers, choosing between writing a memoir and an autobiography depends on what aspects of their life they wish to share and how they want to share them. If they aim to provide a comprehensive account of their life, with a focus on factual recounting of events, an autobiography may be the suitable format. However, if they wish to share a more personal and thematic exploration of their life experiences, a memoir would be more appropriate.

Understanding the nuances between memoirs and autobiographies allows writers to effectively frame and communicate their life stories, ensuring that their narratives not only capture their personal journeys but also resonate with their readers in a meaningful way.

THE POWER OF MEMORY: RECALLING AND RECORDING

Memory plays a pivotal role in the creation of a memoir. It is the reservoir from which writers draw their stories, but it is also a complex and often elusive element of the human mind. The act of recalling and recording memories for a memoir involves navigating the intricacies of memory, understanding its malleability, and finding ways to authentically capture past experiences.

Understanding the Nature of Memory

Memory is not a static or infallible record of the past. It is dynamic and can be influenced by various factors, such as emotions, subsequent experiences, and the passage of time. Memories can fade, change, or even be reconstructed. This fluid nature of memory poses a challenge for memoir writers, who must discern the essence of their past experiences while acknowledging the potential for distortion.

Techniques for Recalling Memories

1. **Sensory Recall**: Engaging the senses can be a powerful way to access memories. Smells, sounds, and sights

can trigger recollections that might otherwise remain hidden. Writers can revisit old photographs, listen to music from the past, or engage in activities that were part of their earlier experiences.

2. **Writing Prompts**: Using prompts can stimulate memory recall. These can be specific questions about the past, lists of significant life events, or explorations of relationships and places. Responding to prompts can unearth memories that are not immediately accessible.

3. **Interviews and Conversations**: Talking with friends, family, or others who shared in past experiences can help jog memory and offer different perspectives on the same events. These conversations can fill gaps in memory and provide a more rounded understanding of past events.

Recording Memories with Honesty and Clarity

Once memories are recalled, the challenge lies in recording them in a way that is both honest and clear. Memoir writers must balance their subjective recollections with a commitment to truthful storytelling.

- **Acknowledging Subjectivity**: Memoirists should recognize and, where appropriate, disclose the subjective nature of their memories. This honesty enhances the credibility of the narrative and acknowledges the complex nature of personal history.

- **Using Descriptive Detail**: Detailed descriptions can bring memories to life, helping readers visualize and empathize with the past experiences being recounted. These details should be as accurate as possible, but also reflective of the writer's personal perception of events.

- **Exploring Emotional Truths**: Beyond factual accuracy, memoirs should aim to capture the emotional truth of past experiences. How events felt, the impact they had, and the lessons learned are often more significant than the precise details of the events themselves.

The process of recalling and recording memories is a key aspect of memoir writing. It involves not just the retrieval of past experiences but also an examination of their meanings and the emotions they evoke. By navigating the complexities of memory with honesty and introspection, memoir writers can create narratives that not only recount their life stories but also resonate with the broader truths of human experience.

HONING YOUR NARRATIVE VOICE

Developing a unique narrative voice is a fundamental aspect of memoir writing. This voice serves as the medium through which the story is told, reflecting the author's personality, perspective, and style. A well-crafted narrative voice can enhance the reader's engagement with the memoir, making the story more compelling and relatable.

Understanding Narrative Voice

Narrative voice is the persona through which a story is told. It encompasses the tone, style, and perspective of the narration. In memoirs, the narrative voice is deeply personal, as it represents the author's way of seeing and interpreting their experiences. It's not just about how the story is told, but also about who is telling it and from what viewpoint.

Elements of a Strong Narrative Voice

1. **Authenticity**: The voice in a memoir should be authentically the author's own. It should reflect their true personality and way of expressing themselves, not an imitation of someone else's style or what they think readers want to hear.
2. **Consistency**: A consistent voice helps in maintaining

the flow of the narrative and keeping the reader engaged. While the tone may shift depending on the content, the underlying voice should remain recognizable and steady throughout the memoir.

3. **Clarity and Accessibility**: The voice should be clear and accessible to the reader. It should convey the author's thoughts and experiences in a way that is understandable and relatable, without being overly complex or convoluted.

Developing Your Narrative Voice

1. **Reflect on Your Speaking Style**: One way to find your narrative voice is to consider how you speak in everyday life. What words do you use? What's your typical tone? Incorporating elements of your natural speaking style can bring authenticity to your writing voice.

2. **Read Widely**: Exposure to a variety of writing styles can help in identifying what resonates with you and what doesn't. As you read, pay attention to how different authors convey their voices and what elements you might want to adopt or avoid in your own writing.

3. **Write Regularly**: Like any skill, developing a narrative voice takes practice. Regular writing, whether through journaling, blogging, or drafting your memoir, helps in refining your voice. Over time, you'll become more comfortable in your writing and more attuned to your unique style.

4. **Seek Feedback**: Getting feedback from trusted readers can provide valuable insights into how your voice is perceived and areas where it can be strengthened or made more consistent.

Experimenting with Voice

Experimentation can also play a role in developing your narrative voice. Trying out different styles, tones, and perspectives can help you discover what feels most natural and effective for your memoir. This experimentation can involve writing the same story from different viewpoints, playing with various tones (humorous, serious, reflective), or experimenting with different narrative structures.

Developing a narrative voice in memoir writing is a process of exploration and refinement. It involves understanding the elements that make a voice compelling, consistent, and authentic, and then applying these in a way that best suits the story you want to tell. A well-crafted narrative voice not only engages readers but also adds depth and personality to the memoir, making it a unique reflection of the author's life and experiences.

PART II: BRAIN TO PAPER – STRUCTURING, DEVELOPMENT AND OVERCOMING OBSTACLES

Structuring Your Memoir

The structure of a memoir is a crucial element that shapes the way the story unfolds and how it is received by readers.

A well-structured memoir enhances readability, maintains engagement, and helps convey the message and themes of the narrative effectively. There are various structures that memoirists can choose from, each offering different ways of presenting life stories.

Traditional Chronological Structure

The chronological structure is the most straightforward approach, where events are narrated in the order they occurred. This linear progression can be easy for readers to follow and provides a clear sequence of how events have shaped the author's life. However, it also requires careful pacing to maintain interest, especially during less dramatic periods.

Thematic Structure

In a thematic structure, the memoir is organized around specific themes or subjects rather than the sequence of events. This approach allows the writer to delve deeply into particular aspects of their life, such as family relationships, career development, or personal challenges. The thematic structure can make the memoir more reflective and analytical.

Reflective or Essayistic Structure

A reflective or essayistic structure focuses on the author's introspection and commentary about their experiences. Rather than following a strict chronological or thematic order, this structure weaves together narrative and reflection, allowing the author to ponder the significance of their experiences and share insights with the reader.

Fragmented or Non-Linear Structure

Some memoirs adopt a fragmented or non-linear structure, where the narrative is presented out of chronological order or broken into discrete sections that may not immediately seem connected. This structure can create a sense of mystery or intrigue, engaging the reader in piecing together the narrative. It can also reflect the unpredictable and disjointed nature of memory and experience.

Interwoven Storylines

Memoirs with interwoven storylines may alternate between different periods in the author's life or between different characters or viewpoints. This approach can provide a more dynamic and multifaceted view of the author's experiences and can highlight contrasts or parallels between different aspects of their life.

Choosing the Right Structure

Selecting the right structure for a memoir depends on the story the author wants to tell and how they wish to engage their readers. Factors to consider include the nature of the experiences being shared, the themes the author wishes to highlight, and the emotional journey they want to take the reader on. It's important to choose a structure that complements the content of the memoir and enhances the narrative's impact.

Flexibility in Structure

Memoirists should also feel free to be flexible with their chosen structure. It's not uncommon for the structure of a memoir to evolve during the writing process as the narrative develops and new themes or connections emerge. This flexibility can lead to a more organic and authentic narrative.

In memoir writing, structure is more than just a framework for organizing content; it is a tool for shaping the narrative and guiding the reader's journey through the story. A well-chosen structure can add depth and meaning to the memoir, helping to turn a personal history into a compelling, thoughtful, and engaging narrative.

THE ETHICS OF MEMOIR WRITING

Navigating the ethical landscape in memoir writing involves a delicate balance between truth-telling and respect for the privacy and dignity of others featured in the narrative. Memoirists face unique ethical challenges as they recount real-life experiences that often involve other people. Addressing these challenges requires careful consideration and a commitment to ethical principles in writing.

Balancing Truth and Privacy

One of the primary ethical considerations in memoir writing is balancing the writer's commitment to truth with the need to respect the privacy of others. Memoirists often share personal and sometimes intimate details about their lives, which can include sensitive information about friends, family, and acquaintances.

- **Seeking Permission**: Where possible, it's advisable to seek permission from individuals who play significant roles in the narrative. This practice not only respects their privacy but can also prevent potential legal issues.
- **Anonymization**: In cases where obtaining permission is not possible or appropriate, changing names and identifying details can protect the privacy

of individuals without compromising the story's integrity.

Handling Sensitive Topics

Memoirs often delve into sensitive or difficult topics, such as trauma, abuse, or family secrets. Handling these topics requires a sensitive approach that considers the potential impact on both the subjects involved and the readers.

- **Tactful Narration**: When writing about sensitive topics, it's important to do so with care and tact. This might mean avoiding gratuitous details or focusing more on the emotional truth of the experience rather than explicit descriptions.
- **Acknowledging Multiple Perspectives**: Recognizing that each person's experience of shared events can be different is important. Memoirists should acknowledge the subjectivity of their perspective and, where relevant, the possibility of other viewpoints.

Navigating Fiction and Truth

Memoirs, by definition, are rooted in truth. However, the act of remembering and writing about the past inherently involves some degree of interpretation and reconstruction.

- **Admitting Memory's Fallibility**: It's ethical for memoirists to acknowledge the fallibility of memory. This can be addressed in the narrative, reminding readers that while the story is based on true events, the way they are remembered and recounted is subject to the imperfections of memory.
- **Avoiding Deliberate Fictionalization**: While some

degree of interpretation is inevitable, deliberately altering facts or inventing events breaches the ethical pact between the memoirist and the reader. The memoir should remain as truthful as possible to the writer's recollections and understanding of events.

The Writer's Responsibility

Memoirists have a responsibility to their readers, their subjects, and themselves. This responsibility includes being honest, fair, and respectful in their storytelling. It also involves being aware of the potential impact of their narrative on others and handling the stories they tell with care and integrity.

Ethics in memoir writing is a complex and nuanced aspect of the genre. It requires writers to navigate the sometimes conflicting demands of honesty, privacy, sensitivity, and artistic expression. By adhering to ethical practices, memoirists can tell their stories in a way that is both truthful and respectful, ensuring their work is not only compelling but also conscientious.

OVERCOMING WRITER'S BLOCK

Writer's block is a common challenge faced by memoirists, characterized by a temporary inability to proceed with the writing process. It can stem from various sources, such as self-doubt, perfectionism, emotional hurdles, or simply not knowing how to proceed with the narrative. Overcoming writer's block involves understanding its causes and applying strategies to navigate through it.

Identifying the Causes

Understanding the root cause of writer's block is the first step towards overcoming it. For memoirists, common causes include:

- **Emotional Barriers**: Writing a memoir often means delving into deeply personal and sometimes painful experiences, which can bring up emotional barriers to writing.
- **Perfectionism**: The desire to make every sentence perfect can hinder the writing process, leading to a fear of putting words on the page.
- **Lack of Clarity**: Uncertainty about what to include in the memoir or how to structure it can result in writer's block.

Strategies to Overcome Writer's Block

1. **Set Manageable Goals**: Breaking the writing process into small, achievable goals can make the task seem less daunting and help build momentum.
2. **Establish a Routine**: Setting aside regular time for writing and creating a conducive writing environment can foster a habit and make it easier to get into the writing mindset.
3. **Free Writing**: Engaging in free writing sessions, where you write without worrying about quality or relevance to the memoir, can help overcome the fear of imperfection and stimulate creativity.
4. **Change of Scenery**: Sometimes, a change in the writing environment can refresh the mind and provide new inspiration.
5. **Talk About It**: Discussing the memoir and any challenges with friends, family, or writing groups can provide new perspectives and ideas, helping to overcome blocks.
6. **Read and Research**: Reading other memoirs or conducting research relevant to your own can provide inspiration and motivation to continue writing.
7. **Physical Activity**: Engaging in physical activity can clear the mind and reduce stress, potentially easing writer's block.

Addressing Emotional Challenges

Since memoir writing is often personal and emotional, addressing any underlying emotional challenges is important. This might involve:

- **Reflecting on Personal Readiness**: Assessing whether you're emotionally ready to write about certain experiences and giving yourself permission to leave some stories untold if they are too painful.
- **Seeking Support**: Consulting with a therapist or counselor can provide emotional support and tools to navigate through difficult memories and experiences.

Accepting Imperfection

Acceptance of imperfection in the initial stages of writing can be liberating. First drafts are rarely perfect, and accepting this can alleviate the pressure to write flawlessly, allowing the words to flow more freely.

Overcoming writer's block in memoir writing is not just about finding ways to continue writing, but also about understanding and addressing the unique challenges that come with narrating one's life story. By employing effective strategies and being mindful of the emotional aspects of memoir writing, writers can navigate through these blocks and continue on their journey of storytelling.

WRITING WITH HONESTY AND VULNERABILITY

Writing a memoir with honesty and vulnerability is essential for creating a powerful and relatable narrative. This approach involves delving into the depths of personal experiences and emotions, presenting them in a raw and unfiltered manner. It requires courage and introspection, as the writer exposes their vulnerabilities to the reader, creating a bond of trust and empathy.

Embracing Honesty in Memoir Writing

Honesty is the cornerstone of memoir writing. It entails being truthful about events, feelings, and reflections. This truth is not just about factual accuracy; it's about emotional honesty – expressing genuine feelings and reactions, even if they reveal flaws, mistakes, or weaknesses.

- **Facing Uncomfortable Truths**: Writing honestly often means confronting uncomfortable aspects of one's past, including failures, regrets, or painful experiences. It's about acknowledging these truths and presenting them without self-censorship.
- **Resisting the Urge to Idealize**: Memoirists should

avoid the temptation to present themselves or others in an idealized light. Life is complex, and a memoir should reflect the multifaceted nature of human experiences and relationships.

The Power of Vulnerability

Vulnerability in writing goes hand in hand with honesty. It involves opening up about personal struggles, doubts, and fears. By showing vulnerability, memoirists connect with readers on a deeper level, as they see reflections of their own vulnerabilities in the narrative.

- **Sharing Personal Struggles**: Writing about personal struggles, whether they are emotional, physical, or mental, can be daunting but also deeply cathartic. It invites readers to engage with the memoir on a more intimate level.

- **Emotional Transparency**: Being transparent about one's emotions is a way to show vulnerability. This transparency allows readers to understand the depth of the writer's experiences and the journey they have undergone.

Navigating the Risks

While honesty and vulnerability are powerful tools, they also come with risks. Memoirists must navigate the fine line between openness and oversharing, ensuring that their narrative remains respectful and considerate of themselves and others involved.

- **Maintaining Personal Boundaries**: It's important to establish what aspects of one's life are open for discussion and what remains private. These boundaries are crucial for the writer's well-being.

- **Considering the Impact on Others**: Memoirists should also consider how their honesty and vulnerability might affect others featured in their stories. Balancing truth-telling with respect for others' privacy and dignity is a key aspect of ethical memoir writing.

Writing with honesty and vulnerability requires a delicate balance between openness and discretion. By embracing these qualities, memoirists can craft narratives that are not only compelling and authentic but also resonate with readers on a deeply personal level. This approach fosters a connection that transcends the pages of the memoir, leaving a lasting impact on both the writer and the reader.

CRAFTING COMPELLING OPENINGS

The opening of a memoir sets the tone for the entire narrative and is crucial in capturing the reader's interest. A compelling opening not only introduces the story but also hooks the reader, compelling them to continue on the journey with the author. It can be a daunting task, as it carries the weight of making a strong first impression.

A successful opening in memoir writing often includes elements that immediately engage the reader. This could be a vivid scene, a poignant memory, an intriguing statement, or a moment of tension or conflict. The goal is to draw the reader into the world of the memoir right from the start.

Establishing a Connection from the Beginning

The opening should establish a connection with the reader. This connection can be emotional, intellectual, or curiosity-driven. By presenting a relatable, intriguing, or emotionally resonant moment, memoirists invite readers into their life story. This moment should give a glimpse into the themes or experiences that will be explored in greater depth throughout the memoir.

Setting the Scene

Descriptive and evocative scene-setting can be a powerful tool in a memoir's opening. It situates the reader in a specific time and place, providing a backdrop against which the story will unfold. The description should be vivid enough to transport the reader but not so detailed as to overwhelm the narrative thrust.

Introducing the Narrative Voice

The opening is also an opportunity to introduce the memoir's narrative voice. This voice should be distinct, conveying the author's unique perspective and personality. The way the story is told - whether with humor, solemnity, or lyrical prose - can significantly influence how the reader engages with the narrative.

Presenting a Hook

A strong hook is essential in a memoir's opening. This hook could be a question, a surprising fact, a challenging statement, or an intriguing scene that piques the reader's interest. It should create a sense of curiosity or urgency that compels the reader to keep turning the pages.

Reflecting the Core Themes

While the opening should be engaging, it should also be reflective of the memoir's core themes and tone. It should provide a preview of what the memoir will explore, whether it's a journey of self-discovery, a tale of overcoming adversity, or a reflection on a significant period or event in the author's life.

The opening of a memoir is more than just the start of a story; it's an invitation into the author's world. By crafting an opening that is engaging, evocative, and reflective of the memoir's themes and voice, writers can capture the interest of their readers and set the stage for a compelling narrative journey.

DEVELOPING CHARACTERS IN MEMOIRS

In memoir writing, the portrayal of characters, including oneself, is a critical aspect. These characters are real people, and their representation in the narrative plays a significant role in how the story is perceived and related to by readers. Developing characters in a memoir involves a blend of factual accuracy, emotional depth, and narrative engagement.

Portraying Real People

When writing about real people, it's important to balance respect for their real-life counterparts with the needs of the narrative. Memoirists should strive for honesty in their portrayals while being mindful of privacy and ethical considerations. This involves a thoughtful approach to how much detail to include and how to present the interactions and relationships that shape the story.

The Memoirist as a Character

In memoirs, the author is often the central character. This self-portrayal requires introspection and self-awareness. Writers need to present themselves with a level of objectivity, acknowledging their flaws and growth throughout the story. It's about being authentic and showing vulnerability, which allows readers to connect with the author on a deeper level.

Depth and Complexity

Characters in memoirs should be presented with depth and complexity. This means going beyond surface descriptions to explore their motivations, emotions, and the impact they have on the memoirist's life. Developing well-rounded portrayals provides the narrative with richness and helps readers understand the interpersonal dynamics that are central to the memoir.

Dialogue and Interaction

Dialogue is a key tool in character development. It can reveal personality, emotion, and relationship dynamics. Using remembered conversations or reconstructed dialogue can bring characters to life and add authenticity to their portrayal. However, memoirists should be careful to ensure that dialogue remains true to the character and the essence of what was said, even if it's not a verbatim account.

Reflecting Change and Growth

Characters in a memoir, including the memoirist, often undergo change and growth. Showing this evolution is important for a dynamic narrative. It's about illustrating how experiences and interactions have impacted the characters, leading to personal development or shifts in perspective.

Respecting Privacy

While honesty is important in character portrayal, so is respecting the privacy of the individuals involved. This might mean altering identifying details or seeking permission from those who play significant roles in the narrative. Being sensitive to how others are portrayed and the potential impact on their lives is a key consideration in memoir writing.

Developing characters in a memoir is a delicate balance between truthful representation and narrative artistry. It involves presenting real people, including oneself, with honesty, depth, and complexity, while being mindful of the ethical implications of writing about real lives. By doing so, memoirists can create a narrative that is not only engaging but also resonant with the authentic experiences and relationships that define their story.

PART III: SETTING, NARRATIVE, DESCRIPTION, DIALOGUE & PACING

The Role of Setting in Your Memoir

Setting in memoir writing is more than just a backdrop; it's an integral part of the story that adds depth, context, and atmosphere. The setting includes the physical locations, cultural environment, and historical period in which the memoir's events take place. Effectively incorporating setting into a memoir enriches the narrative and helps readers immerse themselves in the author's world.

Establishing Time and Place

A well-described setting establishes the time and place of the events in the memoir. This grounding in a specific location and era helps readers visualize where the story unfolds and understand the context in which the events occur. Whether it's a bustling city, a quiet rural town, or a different country, the setting can significantly influence the narrative's tone and mood.

Reflecting Cultural and Social Context

The setting often reflects the cultural and social context of the memoir. It can provide insights into the community, social norms, and historical events that shaped the author's experiences. By painting a vivid picture of the societal backdrop, memoirists can offer readers a deeper understanding of the challenges, expectations, and opportunities they faced.

Using Setting to Enhance Emotional Impact

The physical environment can also be used to enhance the emotional impact of the story. Descriptions of landscapes, weather, buildings, or rooms can mirror the author's emotions and internal states. For instance, a storm might parallel a turbulent period in the author's life, while a serene landscape might reflect a sense of peace or contentment.

Evoking Nostalgia and Memory

Settings in a memoir can evoke nostalgia and trigger memories, both for the author and the reader. Familiar details about a place or time can resonate with readers, allowing them to connect their own experiences and memories with those of the author.

Dynamic Settings

In some memoirs, the setting might change significantly over the course of the narrative, reflecting the author's journey. These changes can signify transitions, growth, or shifts in perspective. The way the author perceives and describes the setting can also evolve, mirroring their changing internal landscape.

Balancing Description with Narrative

While detailed descriptions of the setting can enhance a memoir, it's important to balance these descriptions with the narrative. Overly lengthy or frequent descriptions can interrupt the story's flow. The key is to integrate setting details naturally into the narrative, using them to support and enrich the story rather than overshadow it.

The role of setting in a memoir is multifaceted. It not only grounds the story in a particular time and place but also adds layers of meaning, reflecting the cultural, social, and emotional dimensions of the author's experiences. A well-crafted setting can transform a memoir from a mere recounting of events into a rich, immersive narrative that fully engages the reader in the author's world.

BALANCING NARRATIVE AND REFLECTION

In memoir writing, the balance between narrative and reflection is crucial. This balance involves weaving together the story of what happened (the narrative) with the author's personal reflections on these events. The interplay between these two elements defines the memoir's depth, engaging readers both with the events of the story and with the author's inner journey.

The Narrative Element

The narrative element of a memoir includes the chronological events, the actions of characters, and the outward occurrences that form the story's backbone. It's the part of the memoir that tells readers what happened, offering a window into the author's experiences.

- **Creating a Compelling Plot**: Even though memoirs are based on real life, they need a plot that keeps readers engaged. This means structuring the memoir with a beginning, middle, and end, and including elements of conflict, tension, and resolution.
- **Show, Don't Tell**: Employing the 'show, don't tell' technique in narrative passages helps bring the story

to life. This involves using descriptive language and details to allow readers to visualize and experience events rather than just reading about them.

The Reflective Element

Reflection in memoir writing is where the author steps back to ponder the significance of the events. It's a space for introspection, where the author considers what they learned, how they changed, or what they now understand about themselves and the world.

- **Providing Insight and Perspective**: Reflection gives the memoir depth and meaning. It's an opportunity for the author to share insights, make connections between events, and explore the emotional and psychological aspects of their experiences.
- **Balancing Reflection with Action**: Too much reflection can slow down the narrative, while too little can make the memoir feel superficial. Finding the right balance is key to maintaining the memoir's pace and engagement.

Techniques for Balancing Narrative and Reflection

- **Intersperse Reflection with Action**: One effective technique is to intersperse moments of reflection within the narrative. This allows the story to flow while providing regular pauses for insight and introspection.
- **Reflective Segments at Key Moments**: Placing reflective segments at key moments in the story, such as after a major event or at the end of a chapter, can

provide readers with necessary pauses to digest the narrative and understand its deeper meanings.

- **Varying the Length and Depth of Reflection**: Depending on the importance of the event, reflections can vary in length and depth. Some moments might warrant a deeper introspective dive, while others might need just a brief contemplation.

Balancing narrative and reflection is essential in crafting a memoir that is both engaging and meaningful. It allows memoirists to tell their stories in a way that not only recounts their experiences but also delves into the lessons learned and the personal growth that occurred. This balance ensures that the memoir resonates with readers, offering them not just a story, but a journey through the author's inner landscape.

THE ART OF DESCRIPTIVE WRITING

Descriptive writing in memoirs plays a crucial role in bringing stories to life. It allows readers to visualize the scenes, feel the emotions, and immerse themselves in the experiences narrated. Effective descriptive writing goes beyond merely providing information; it evokes the senses, conveys emotions, and paints a vivid picture of the moments and experiences that have shaped the author's life.

Evoking the Senses

Good descriptive writing engages the reader's senses. Descriptions of sights, sounds, smells, textures, and tastes can transport readers to the moment being described. For example, detailing the scent of rain on dry earth or the sound of laughter in a family gathering can vividly recreate the scene for the reader.

Showing Emotions and Atmosphere

Descriptive writing is also about conveying emotions and atmosphere. How a scene is described can reflect the author's feelings at the time. Describing a setting with a gloomy, overcast sky can mirror a sense of melancholy, while bright, warm sunlight can evoke feelings of joy and optimism.

Using Metaphors and Similes

Metaphors and similes are powerful tools in descriptive writing. They allow writers to make creative comparisons that can be more evocative than direct descriptions. For instance, comparing a difficult period in life to navigating a storm can provide deeper insight into the author's experiences.

Being Specific and Detailed

Specificity and detail are key to effective descriptive writing. General descriptions can fail to engage the reader, while detailed, specific descriptions create a more vivid and relatable image. For example, instead of saying "the garden was beautiful," describing the vibrant colors of the flowers and the patterns of light and shadow can create a more compelling picture.

Balancing Description with Narrative

While descriptive writing is important, it needs to be balanced with the narrative. Overly lengthy descriptions can slow the pace of the memoir and distract from the story. The key is to integrate descriptions naturally into the narrative, using them to enhance the story rather than overshadow it.

Reflecting Personal Perspective

In memoir writing, descriptions should also reflect the author's personal perspective. How the author describes a person, place, or event can give readers insight into their feelings and perceptions, adding depth to the narrative.

The art of descriptive writing in memoirs is about creating a tapestry of words that not only informs but also evokes and resonates. By skillfully weaving descriptive passages into their narrative, memoirists can create a rich, immersive experience that allows readers to fully engage with their stories.

DIALOGUE IN MEMOIRS

Incorporating dialogue into memoirs is a powerful way to bring stories to life. Dialogue allows readers to hear the voices of the characters, adding realism and depth to the narrative. In memoir writing, dialogue serves several functions: it develops characters, advances the plot, and enhances the authenticity of the memoir.

Creating Realistic Dialogue

Dialogue in memoirs should reflect how people actually speak. This means capturing the unique speech patterns, dialects, and idioms of the characters. Realistic dialogue often includes colloquial language and can be less grammatically correct than written prose, which helps to create believable and relatable characters.

Advancing the Narrative

Good dialogue in memoirs does more than just mimic real speech; it also advances the narrative. Through dialogue, memoirists can reveal important information, move the plot forward, and develop conflicts or relationships. Dialogue can be a dynamic way of showing what's happening rather than telling it through descriptive passages.

Revealing Character

Dialogue is a key tool in character development. The way a person speaks can reveal much about their personality, background, and current emotional state. For example, a character's choice of words, tone, and speech rhythm can provide insights into their mood, education level, or cultural background.

Balancing Authenticity and Privacy

When writing dialogue in memoirs, balancing authenticity with respect for privacy is important. While it's impossible to remember every conversation verbatim, memoirists should strive to reproduce the essence and intention of real conversations. If a dialogue could potentially infringe on someone's privacy or be harmful, it's ethical to alter identifying details or seek permission from the individuals involved.

Using Dialogue to Convey Emotion

Dialogue can be an effective way of conveying emotion. How something is said often carries more weight than what is said. The emotional undercurrents of a conversation, conveyed through dialogue, can add depth to the narrative and provide a more immersive experience for the reader.

Dialogue as a Reflection of Time and Place

Dialogue can also reflect the time and place in which the memoir is set. The way people spoke in a specific era or cultural context can add authenticity to the memoir, grounding the narrative in its historical or social setting.

In memoir writing, dialogue is more than just a transcription of spoken words; it's a narrative tool that brings characters to life, advances the story, and adds depth to the memoir. Effective use of dialogue can transform a memoir from a mere recounting of events into a vivid, engaging narrative that resonates with readers.

PACING YOUR STORY

Pacing in memoir writing refers to the speed at which the narrative unfolds and how it holds the reader's attention. Effective pacing is crucial for maintaining reader engagement, creating tension, and developing a rhythmic flow in the story. It involves the careful arrangement of events, reflections, descriptions, and dialogues to create a balanced and compelling narrative.

Understanding the Role of Pacing

Pacing controls the rhythm of the memoir, much like the tempo in music. It determines how quickly or slowly the story progresses and can be used to highlight important moments, build suspense, or provide space for reflection. Good pacing keeps the reader invested in the story, seamlessly guiding them through the various aspects of the memoir.

Variability in Pacing

A memoir does not need to maintain a constant pace. In fact, varying the pace can enhance the narrative by creating contrast and interest. Faster pacing can be used during moments of high action or tension, while slower pacing can be employed in reflective or descriptive passages to allow deeper exploration of thoughts and feelings.

Balancing Action with Reflection

Balancing faster-paced sections with slower, more introspective parts is key to effective pacing. This balance ensures that the memoir provides both the excitement of action and the depth of personal insight. It prevents the narrative from becoming either too rushed and superficial or too slow and introspective.

Using Structure to Influence Pacing

The structure of the memoir can greatly influence its pacing. Short, succinct chapters or sections can quicken the pace, while longer, more detailed ones can slow it down. The arrangement of events and chapters should be strategic, based on the desired impact on the reader and the overall flow of the story.

Controlling Pace with Language and Sentences

The choice of language and sentence structure also affects pacing. Short, direct sentences can quicken the pace and build tension, while longer, more complex sentences can slow down the narrative, offering a more contemplative tone. The use of dialogue, descriptions, and action also plays a role in pacing, with each contributing differently to the speed and rhythm of the narrative.

Adjusting Pace to Enhance Emotional Impact

Pacing can be adjusted to enhance the emotional impact of different sections of the memoir. For instance, slowing down the pace during emotionally charged moments allows readers to fully experience and understand the significance of these events. Conversely, quickening the pace during action-driven scenes can heighten excitement and suspense.

Effective pacing in memoir writing is about finding the right rhythm that aligns with the story's content and the emotional journey of the author. It requires thoughtful consideration of the narrative's structure, language, and the balance between action and reflection. By mastering pacing, memoirists can create a captivating and rhythmically engaging narrative that resonates with readers.

PART IV: THEMES, RESEARCH, SENSITIVITY, ETHICS & HUMOR

Thematic Threads in Memoirs

Thematic threads in memoirs are the underlying themes or central ideas that tie together different stories and reflections within the narrative. These themes provide coherence and deeper meaning to the memoir, allowing the author to connect individual experiences to larger, more universal concepts. Identifying and weaving thematic threads throughout a memoir can transform a collection of personal anecdotes into a compelling and resonant narrative.

Identifying Themes

Themes in a memoir often arise naturally from the author's experiences and reflections. They can be related to personal growth, relationships, struggles, achievements, or broader social and cultural issues. Identifying these themes requires introspection and a deep understanding of what the memoir is fundamentally about.

Weaving Themes Throughout the Narrative

Once identified, these themes should be carefully woven throughout the memoir. This can be done by revisiting these themes at various points in the narrative, linking different stories and reflections to the overarching thematic threads. This repetition and exploration of themes help to reinforce them, making the narrative more cohesive and impactful.

Reflecting on Universal Experiences

Themes in a memoir often resonate with universal experiences, even when they arise from very personal stories. By exploring these universal aspects, the memoir connects the author's individual experiences to the broader human condition, making the story more relatable and impactful for a wider audience.

Using Themes to Structure the Memoir

Themes can also be used to structure the memoir. Instead of a strictly chronological approach, the narrative can be organized around key themes, with different sections or chapters exploring various aspects of these themes. This thematic structure can provide a fresh and engaging way of presenting the memoir.

Themes as a Lens for Reflection

Themes can act as a lens through which the author reflects on their experiences. Instead of merely recounting events, the memoirist can explore how these events speak to larger themes, what lessons were learned, and how these experiences have shaped their understanding and perspective.

Balancing Themes with Personal Narrative

While themes are important, they should not overshadow the personal narrative. The memoir should maintain a balance between exploring these broader themes and telling the author's unique, personal story. The themes should enhance and provide depth to the personal narrative, not detract from it.

Incorporating thematic threads in memoir writing adds depth and coherence to the narrative, elevating it from a personal account to a story with broader resonance. By carefully identifying and weaving these themes throughout their memoir, authors can create a narrative that not only tells their story but also speaks to larger, universal experiences and truths.

RESEARCH AND FACT-CHECKING IN MEMOIRS

Research and fact-checking are crucial components in the process of writing a memoir. Even though memoirs are personal narratives based on the author's memories, ensuring factual accuracy in describing real events, places, and people adds credibility and authenticity to the work. This process involves verifying dates, places, events, and descriptions to align the narrative as closely as possible with reality.

Importance of Accuracy

Accuracy in a memoir is vital for maintaining the trust of the reader. Errors in fact can undermine the reader's confidence in the author and can detract from the overall impact of the memoir. While some minor discrepancies can be expected due to the nature of memory, major inaccuracies or inconsistencies should be avoided.

Conducting Research

Research in memoir writing can take various forms:

- **Historical Context**: Understanding the historical

context of the events described in the memoir can provide background information that enriches the narrative.

- **Geographical Accuracy**: Descriptions of places should be verified for accuracy. This might involve researching the geography or specific characteristics of a location at the time the memoir is set.
- **Cultural Accuracy**: For memoirs set in a culture different from the author's own, or in a past era, it's important to research cultural norms, practices, and language to ensure accurate representation.

Fact-Checking Personal Records

Personal records such as diaries, letters, photographs, and official documents can be invaluable resources for fact-checking in memoir writing. These records can help verify dates, events, and details that might have faded or altered in the author's memory.

Interviews and Personal Accounts

Interviews with people who were part of the events or who can provide additional perspectives can be extremely helpful. These personal accounts can offer insights and details that enhance the authenticity of the memoir.

Ethical Considerations

Fact-checking also involves ethical considerations. It's important to balance the need for accuracy with respect for the privacy and perspectives of others involved in the memoir. In cases where facts are disputed or sensitive, it might be necessary to alter certain details, anonymize individuals, or include a disclaimer about potential inaccuracies.

Dealing with Memory Gaps

In cases where certain details or events cannot be accurately recalled or verified, the author might choose to acknowledge these memory gaps in the narrative. This transparency maintains the authenticity of the memoir while acknowledging the limitations of memory.

Research and fact-checking in memoir writing serve to ground the personal narrative in a framework of factual accuracy and historical authenticity. By dedicating time and effort to this process, memoirists can enhance the credibility and richness of their story, providing readers with a narrative that is not only personal and emotionally truthful but also accurate and reliable in its representation of real events and settings.

ADDRESSING SENSITIVE TOPICS

Writing about sensitive topics in memoirs requires a thoughtful and respectful approach. Sensitive topics can range from personal or family secrets to larger social issues. Tackling these subjects demands a balance between honesty and discretion, ensuring that the narrative remains authentic and impactful without causing unnecessary harm or discomfort to anyone involved, including the author.

Approaching Personal Trauma

When dealing with personal trauma, memoirists should consider their own readiness to share these experiences. Writing about trauma can be cathartic, but it can also reopen old wounds. It's important to prioritize one's emotional well-being and seek support if needed.

Respecting Others Involved

Writing about sensitive topics often involves other people who may be directly or indirectly affected by the narrative. It is crucial to consider their privacy and feelings. This may involve changing names or details, or in some cases, deciding not to include certain information.

Balancing Honesty and Tact

While it's important to be honest in a memoir, it's equally important to be tactful. This means finding ways to tell the truth without being unnecessarily graphic or explicit, especially when dealing with sensitive or potentially triggering topics.

The Impact on Readers

Memoirists should also consider the potential impact of sensitive content on their readers. Including content warnings or choosing not to describe certain events in graphic detail can be ways to respect the boundaries and sensitivities of the audience.

Cultural and Social Sensitivities

When discussing topics that are culturally, socially, or politically sensitive, it's important to approach them with an awareness of the broader context. This involves understanding and acknowledging different perspectives and ensuring that the memoir does not perpetuate stereotypes or misinformation.

Legal Considerations

Sensitive topics can sometimes have legal implications, especially if they involve allegations of criminal activity or defamation. It is advisable to consult legal experts when dealing with such subjects to avoid legal repercussions.

Addressing sensitive topics in memoirs is a complex task that requires careful navigation. By approaching these subjects with empathy, respect, and thoughtfulness, memoirists can write about even the most difficult experiences in a way that is honest and powerful, yet sensitive to the needs and rights of all involved.

THE ROLE OF HUMOR IN MEMOIRS

Incorporating humor into a memoir can be a powerful tool to enhance storytelling, connect with readers, and provide relief from more serious content. Humor in memoirs can serve various purposes: it can humanize the author, make the narrative more engaging, and offer readers a respite from heavy themes. However, using humor effectively in memoir writing requires a delicate balance and an understanding of its impact on the overall tone of the narrative.

Humanizing the Narrative

Humor can make the author more relatable and endearing to readers. Sharing humorous anecdotes or observations allows readers to see the author's lighter, more personable side. This connection is particularly important in memoirs, where the reader's engagement with the author's story is key.

Balancing Seriousness with Levity

Memoirs often deal with serious, sometimes difficult subjects. Humor can provide moments of levity, making the narrative more digestible and less overwhelming for readers. When used appropriately, it can create a balance between the serious and lighter aspects of the story, giving readers an emotional break.

Reflecting on Life's Absurdities

Humor can also be a tool for reflecting on the absurdities and ironies of life. Many memoirists use humor to comment on the peculiarities of their experiences or the world around them. This can add depth to the narrative, allowing readers to see different perspectives on the author's experiences.

Types of Humor in Memoirs

The type of humor used in a memoir can vary greatly depending on the author's style and the story's tone. It can range from subtle wit and dry observations to more overt comedic anecdotes. The key is to choose a style of humor that fits naturally with the narrative and the author's voice.

The Risks of Misusing Humor

While humor can be an effective tool, it also carries risks. Inappropriate or poorly timed humor can alienate readers, especially when dealing with sensitive subjects. It's important for memoirists to be mindful of how their humor might be received and to ensure that it does not undermine the seriousness of their experiences or those of others.

Incorporating humor into a memoir can add warmth, relatability, and engagement to the narrative. When used thoughtfully, it can enhance the storytelling, providing readers with a richer, more nuanced understanding of the author's experiences and perspective.

WRITING ABOUT OTHERS ETHICALLY

Ethical considerations are paramount when writing about others in a memoir. Since memoirs involve real people, writers are tasked with the responsibility of portraying others in a way that is both truthful and respectful. Striking this balance requires a thoughtful approach to how others are depicted, considering the impact of the memoir not only on the subjects themselves but also on their families, friends, and communities.

In the realm of memoir writing, the ethical portrayal of others involves several key aspects. First and foremost is the commitment to truth. This does not mean that every detail of every event needs to be included; rather, it's about ensuring that the essence and context of interactions and relationships are presented honestly.

However, being truthful does not equate to being hurtful or insensitive. Memoirists must navigate the delicate line between honesty and respect for the privacy and dignity of the people in their stories. This often involves making tough decisions about what to include and what to leave out. In some cases, changing names and identifying details can protect privacy while still conveying the story's emotional truth.

Consent is another crucial aspect. Whenever possible, it's advisable to seek permission from the people who play significant roles in the narrative, especially when their stories are deeply intertwined with the author's own. This not only fosters respect and integrity but can also provide additional perspectives that enrich the memoir.

Memoirists also need to be aware of the potential impact of their writing on the individuals involved. This includes considering the emotional, psychological, and, in some cases, legal repercussions that might arise from the memoir's publication.

In dealing with difficult or controversial subjects that involve others, memoirists should aim to be fair and balanced, presenting the events in a way that is reflective of their complexity. This might mean acknowledging different viewpoints or admitting to gaps in memory or understanding.

Ethical writing about others in memoirs is not just about adhering to moral principles; it's about treating the stories of others with the same care and respect as one would treat their own. By doing so, memoirists can create narratives that are not only compelling and truthful but also compassionate and considerate of the real people behind the stories.

PART V: EDITING, AMENDING & REVISING & OVERCOMING PROBLEMS

The Revision Process

The revision process in memoir writing is where the initial draft is transformed into a polished, cohesive narrative. This stage is crucial as it allows the author to refine their story, enhance clarity, and ensure the memoir effectively conveys its themes and messages. Revision involves multiple layers, from addressing big-picture issues to fine-tuning language and grammar.

Big-Picture Revisions

Initially, the focus should be on big-picture elements. This includes the overall structure of the memoir, the flow of the narrative, and the consistency of themes and voice. Authors should assess whether the memoir's structure effectively supports the story, if transitions between different sections are smooth, and whether the thematic threads are consistently woven throughout the narrative.

Character and Setting Development

Another key aspect is the development of characters and settings. During revision, authors have the opportunity to deepen the portrayal of characters, including themselves, ensuring they are multidimensional and authentic. Similarly, settings can be revisited to add more vivid and descriptive details, enhancing the reader's immersion in the story.

Refining Language and Style

Language and style refinement are also critical. This involves fine-tuning the memoir's voice, ensuring it is consistent and authentic throughout. Authors should also pay attention to the rhythm of their writing, the use of literary devices, and the overall readability of the text.

Clarity and Conciseness

Ensuring clarity and conciseness is vital. The memoir should communicate its story and themes clearly, without unnecessary digressions or overly complex language. This might involve cutting redundant passages, simplifying convoluted sentences, or clarifying ambiguous sections.

Feedback and Receptive Editing

Seeking feedback from trusted readers, writing groups, or professional editors can be invaluable. External perspectives can highlight areas that need improvement, which might not be apparent to the author. Being receptive to constructive criticism and willing to make changes based on feedback is essential for effective revision.

The Final Polish

The last step in the revision process is the final polish. This includes proofreading for grammar, spelling, and punctuation errors. Ensuring the manuscript is error-free is important as it reflects on the professionalism and quality of the memoir.

Revision is an integral part of the memoir writing process. It requires time, patience, and a critical eye. By thoroughly revising their work, authors can ensure their memoir is engaging, coherent, and a true reflection of their story and artistic vision.

OVERCOMING SELF-DOUBT AND CRITICISM

Writing a memoir often involves facing self-doubt and criticism, both from oneself and from others. These challenges can act as significant barriers to writing and sharing one's story. Developing strategies to manage and overcome these doubts and criticisms is essential for memoirists to ensure their stories are told with authenticity and confidence.

Understanding the Sources of Self-Doubt

Self-doubt in memoir writing can stem from various sources. It might be the fear of exposing personal aspects of one's life, concern about how others will perceive the story, or simply the inner critic questioning the writer's ability to tell their story effectively. Recognizing the sources of these doubts is the first step in addressing them.

Techniques to Counter Self-Doubt

- **Affirmation and Positive Reinforcement**: Regularly affirming one's worth and the value of one's story can be a powerful counter to self-doubt. This might involve reminding oneself of the unique perspectives and experiences that make the story worth telling.

- **Setting Realistic Expectations**: Understanding that no piece of writing is perfect and that every writer has strengths and weaknesses can help set more realistic expectations and reduce self-criticism.
- **Building a Support System**: Engaging with a supportive community of fellow writers, friends, or family members can provide encouragement and constructive feedback, helping to mitigate self-doubt.

Dealing with External Criticism

- **Distinguishing Constructive from Destructive Criticism**: It's important to differentiate between criticism that is constructive and meant to improve the work and criticism that is simply destructive or unhelpful. Embracing the former while disregarding the latter can be beneficial for personal growth and the memoir's development.
- **Staying True to One's Vision**: While being open to feedback, memoirists should also stay true to their vision for their story. Not all criticism needs to be acted upon, especially if it conflicts with the core message and purpose of the memoir.

Strengthening Confidence in Writing

- **Regular Practice**: Writing regularly can build confidence in one's writing abilities. Over time, consistent writing practice can help diminish the power of the inner critic.

- **Education and Improvement**: Engaging in writing courses, workshops, or reading extensively can improve writing skills, thereby boosting confidence.
- **Celebrating Progress and Achievements**: Recognizing and celebrating each step of progress, no matter how small, can reinforce a positive mindset and a sense of accomplishment.

Overcoming self-doubt and criticism is a critical aspect of the memoir writing journey. By developing strategies to manage these challenges, writers can cultivate the resilience and confidence needed to share their stories authentically and courageously.

FINDING INSPIRATION AND STAYING MOTIVATED

Maintaining inspiration and motivation throughout the process of writing a memoir can be challenging. It often involves long periods of introspection, writing, and revision, which can lead to moments of stagnation or a lack of creative drive. Understanding how to continually find inspiration and stay motivated is essential for memoirists to see their projects through to completion.

Cultivating a Routine for Inspiration

Establishing a consistent writing routine can help in maintaining both inspiration and motivation. Setting aside dedicated time for writing, creating a conducive writing environment, and establishing writing rituals can all contribute to a productive writing practice. Regular writing not only fosters discipline but also keeps the creative juices flowing, making it easier to tap into inspiration.

Drawing from Varied Sources of Inspiration

Inspiration for writing a memoir can come from a variety of sources. Reading other memoirs or works of literature, engaging with art or music, and participating in writing groups or workshops can provide new ideas and perspectives. Additionally, everyday experiences, personal relationships, and reflections on past events can also serve as rich sources of inspiration.

Setting Goals and Celebrating Milestones

Setting clear, achievable goals can be a powerful motivator. These goals could range from writing a certain number of words daily to completing a chapter by a specific date. Celebrating milestones, no matter how small, can provide a sense of accomplishment and encourage continued progress.

Overcoming Creative Blocks

Encountering creative blocks is a common experience in memoir writing. When faced with such blocks, changing one's approach can be helpful. This might involve switching to a different section of the memoir, trying a new writing style, or taking a short break from writing to recharge. Sometimes, stepping away from the work momentarily can provide fresh perspectives and renewed inspiration.

Seeking External Motivation

External sources of motivation, such as feedback from peers, writing coaches, or mentors, can provide encouragement and valuable insights. Joining writing communities or participating in writing challenges can also offer support and motivation from fellow writers.

Maintaining inspiration and motivation in memoir writing is a dynamic process that requires flexibility, persistence, and a willingness to seek out and embrace diverse sources of creative stimulation. By cultivating a supportive writing practice and environment, setting achievable goals, and being open to new sources of inspiration, memoirists can sustain their creative momentum and bring their stories to life.

PART VI: ELEVATING YOUR CONTENT & KEY CONSIDERATIONS

The Use of Photographs and Documents

Incorporating photographs and documents into a memoir can greatly enhance the narrative, providing tangible evidence of the experiences and people being written about. These elements add a layer of authenticity and can help to anchor the memoir in reality, offering readers a more immersive and engaging experience.

Enhancing Narrative with Visual Elements

Photographs and documents can serve as powerful visual tools in a memoir. They can provide readers with a direct visual connection to the events and people being described, making the story more relatable and vivid. Photos of people, places, and events, as well as documents like letters, journal entries, or newspaper clippings, can add depth and context to the narrative.

Selecting Relevant Visuals

The selection of photographs and documents to include in a memoir should be intentional and relevant to the story being told. Each visual element should contribute to the narrative or help to illustrate a point. It's important to choose images and documents that complement the text and add meaning to the memoir.

Balancing Text and Visuals

While photographs and documents can enrich a memoir, they should be balanced with the text. Overloading the narrative with too many visual elements can be overwhelming and detract from the story. A thoughtful balance between text and visuals ensures that each enhances the other, providing a cohesive and compelling narrative.

Ethical Considerations

When using photographs and documents, especially those involving other people, ethical considerations should be taken into account. It's important to respect the privacy and rights of individuals who may be depicted or mentioned. In some cases, obtaining permission from the people involved or their families may be necessary.

Captioning and Contextualization

Providing captions or contextual information for photographs and documents can enhance their impact. Captions can include details about the time, place, or people in the image, as well as how they relate to the narrative. This contextualization helps readers understand the significance of the visuals in relation to the memoir.

Incorporating photographs and documents into a memoir is a creative way to deepen the reader's engagement with the story. By carefully selecting and integrating these visual elements, memoirists can create a richer, more layered narrative that provides a unique and personal glimpse into their experiences.

CRAFTING A SATISFYING CONCLUSION

Writing a satisfying conclusion to a memoir is a crucial part of the storytelling process. The conclusion serves to tie together the narrative threads, reflect on the journey, and leave the reader with a lasting impression. It is the place where the author can underscore the central themes, impart final reflections, and perhaps provide a sense of closure to their story.

Reflecting on the Journey

The conclusion is an opportunity for memoirists to reflect on their journey. This reflection could involve considering how they have changed or what they have learned through the experiences narrated in the memoir. It's a chance to look back on the narrative arc and understand its significance in the larger context of the author's life.

Emphasizing Key Themes

In the conclusion, reinforcing the key themes of the memoir is important. This could involve revisiting the main ideas or insights that have been explored throughout the narrative. It's a way to ensure that the themes resonate with the reader long after they finish the book.

Providing Closure

While some memoirs may end with a definitive sense of closure, others might adopt a more open-ended approach. The type of closure provided will depend on the story and the author's intent. In either case, the conclusion should leave the reader feeling satisfied that they have completed a meaningful journey with the author.

Looking to the Future

Some memoirists choose to conclude their memoirs by looking to the future. This might involve contemplating future aspirations, ongoing challenges, or the next phase of the author's journey. It can provide a sense of continuity beyond the pages of the memoir.

The Memoir's Lasting Message

The final words of a memoir are particularly impactful and should be carefully chosen. They are what the reader will remember most vividly. This is the author's opportunity to leave the reader with a lasting message, a final thought that encapsulates the essence of the memoir.

A well-crafted conclusion brings the memoir to a fulfilling end, leaving the reader with a deeper understanding of the author's experiences and insights. It's an essential element that encapsulates the memoir's purpose and provides a resonant and meaningful closure to the narrative journey.

LEGAL CONSIDERATIONS IN MEMOIR WRITING

When writing a memoir, it's important to be aware of the legal considerations that come with publishing a personal story, especially when it involves real people and events. Navigating the legal landscape is crucial to protect both the author and the subjects of the memoir.

Defamation and Libel

One of the primary legal concerns in memoir writing is the risk of defamation or libel. Defamation involves making false statements about a person that could harm their reputation. To avoid potential legal issues, memoirists should ensure that all statements about others are either demonstrably true, opinions, or presented in a way that cannot be proven false.

Right to Privacy

Individuals have a right to privacy, and memoirists need to be cautious not to infringe upon this right. This is particularly pertinent when delving into sensitive or private aspects of other people's lives. In some cases, it might be necessary to alter identifying details or seek permission from the people involved.

Copyright and Intellectual Property

Memoirists should be careful when including copyrighted material, such as song lyrics, poems, or excerpts from published works. Even if these elements played a significant role in the author's life, their inclusion in the memoir without permission could lead to copyright infringement issues.

Contracts and Publishing Agreements

Understanding the terms of publishing agreements is important. Memoirists should be aware of their rights and obligations under these contracts, particularly concerning how the book will be marketed and distributed, and any legal liabilities that the author might bear.

Seeking Legal Advice

Given the potential legal complexities, seeking advice from a legal professional knowledgeable in publishing and media law is advisable. This can provide guidance on how to navigate these issues and reduce the risk of legal challenges after publication.

Navigating the legal aspects of memoir writing is essential for protecting both the author and those featured in the memoir. By understanding and addressing these legal considerations, memoirists can share their personal stories with greater confidence and security.

PART VII: THE PERSONAL IMPACT OF MEMOIR WRITING

The Healing Power of Writing Memoirs

Writing a memoir can be a deeply therapeutic and transformative experience. It allows authors to reflect on their life experiences, process emotions, and find meaning in the events that have shaped them. The act of writing a memoir can offer significant psychological benefits, contributing to the author's personal growth and healing journey.

Processing Life Experiences

Memoir writing provides an opportunity for authors to delve into their past and re-examine their life experiences. This process can be a form of self-therapy, allowing authors to understand and process events and emotions that may have been previously unresolved or unexplored. Writing about these experiences can help in making sense of them, leading to new insights and perspectives.

Finding a Voice

For many memoirists, writing their story is a way to find and assert their voice. This can be particularly empowering for those who have felt silenced or marginalized. Expressing their truth through a memoir allows authors to reclaim their narrative and share their experiences on their own terms.

Connecting with Others

Memoirs often resonate with readers who have had similar experiences, creating a sense of connection and solidarity. For authors, knowing that their stories might help others feel less alone or more understood can be a powerful motivator and a source of comfort. This sense of connection can be incredibly healing, both for the author and the readers.

Catharsis and Release

The act of writing about difficult or emotional experiences can be cathartic. Putting feelings and experiences into words can help release pent-up emotions and lead to a sense of relief or liberation. It can be a way to let go of past burdens and move forward.

Personal Growth and Understanding

Memoir writing often leads to personal growth and increased self-understanding. Reflecting on one's life story can provide clarity about personal values, strengths, and areas for development. It can also offer a greater understanding of the events and people that have influenced the author's life.

The healing power of writing memoirs lies in the opportunity it provides for introspection, expression, and connection. By turning their life stories into memoirs, authors can embark on a journey of self-discovery and healing, finding meaning and resilience in their experiences.

MEMOIR WRITING AS A LEGACY

The act of writing a memoir extends beyond the personal fulfillment it brings; it serves as a legacy for both the author and the readers. Memoirs provide a tangible record of individual experiences and perspectives, offering future generations a glimpse into the author's life, thoughts, and times. This legacy aspect of memoir writing adds a layer of significance and responsibility to the craft.

Preserving Personal Histories

Memoirs are a means of preserving personal histories. They capture the nuances of the author's life, including their experiences, emotions, and the historical and cultural contexts in which they lived. These personal narratives contribute to the broader tapestry of human history, providing detailed and intimate insights that are often absent from traditional historical records.

Impact on Future Generations

Memoirs have the potential to impact future generations. They offer lessons, wisdom, and insights gleaned from the author's experiences. For family members and descendants, a memoir can be a cherished connection to the past, offering a deeper understanding of their heritage and lineage.

Universal Themes and Shared Humanity

While memoirs are deeply personal, they often touch on universal themes and experiences, resonating with a wide audience. This shared humanity aspect allows readers from diverse backgrounds to find aspects of their own life reflected in someone else's story. The memoir then becomes more than just a personal account; it transforms into a shared narrative that contributes to a collective understanding of the human experience.

The legacy of a memoir lies in its power to connect the past, present, and future. It allows the author to leave a lasting imprint, sharing their life story with current and future readers, and contributing to a deeper understanding of the varied tapestry of human lives. Writing a memoir, therefore, is not just an act of personal reflection but also a contribution to the collective memory and history.

PART VIII: MASTERING ADVANCED WRITING TECHNIQUES

Advanced Character Development Techniques

Delving deeper into advanced character development techniques is essential for memoir writers seeking to enrich their narratives and provide readers with a more immersive and emotionally resonant experience. Character development is not just about portraying people accurately; it's about bringing them to life on the page, making them complex, relatable, and memorable. This process involves a nuanced understanding of human nature, motivations, and emotions, as well as the ability to translate these aspects into compelling writing.

Layered Character Portrayal

Advanced character development in memoirs requires a layered approach. Characters, including the author as the central character, should be presented in all their complexity, with their virtues, flaws, contradictions, and transformations. This involves going beyond surface descriptions to explore the depths of their personalities, motivations, and the impact of their experiences.

One effective technique is showing characters in different lights and situations. This not only adds depth but also helps in portraying them as multifaceted individuals. By presenting varied aspects of a character's personality through different interactions and circumstances, memoirists can avoid one-dimensional portrayals.

Emotional Depth and Relatability

Creating emotional depth in characters is crucial for reader engagement. This involves delving into the internal emotional landscapes of the characters, exploring their inner conflicts, fears, hopes, and desires. Memoirists can achieve this by reflecting on and articulating the emotional responses of characters to various situations.

Relatability is another important aspect of character development. Characters should evoke empathy or resonance in readers. This can be achieved by highlighting universal experiences or emotions, even in the midst of unique or extraordinary circumstances. When readers see aspects of their own lives and feelings mirrored in the characters, a deeper connection is established.

Dynamic Character Arcs

In memoir writing, showcasing the evolution of characters is fundamental. Characters should undergo some form of change or growth throughout the narrative. This evolution, known as the character arc, is what makes the journey worthwhile and satisfying for readers. It involves tracking how characters are transformed by their experiences, decisions, and interactions.

Memoirists can illustrate character arcs by juxtaposing past and present perspectives, showing how characters have evolved over time. This contrast between 'then' and 'now' can be a powerful way to demonstrate growth and change.

Utilizing Dialogue and Interaction

Dialogue is an effective tool for character development. Through conversations, memoirists can reveal a character's thought process, personality, and relationship dynamics. The way characters speak, what they choose to say, and what they withhold can all provide insights into their character.

Interactions between characters are also crucial in character development. These interactions can reveal aspects of a character that might not be evident in isolation. How characters react to each other, resolve conflicts, and communicate can tell the reader a lot about their personalities and relationships.

Ethical Considerations

In memoirs, ethical considerations in character development are paramount. Given that characters are real people, memoirists need to balance honesty and empathy. While it's important to portray characters truthfully, it's equally important to treat their stories with respect and sensitivity. This might involve altering certain details, focusing on the emotional truth rather than factual accuracy, or obtaining consent from the individuals involved.

Advanced character development in memoir writing is a nuanced and multifaceted process. It requires an in-depth exploration of characters, a focus on emotional depth and relatability, and an understanding of the transformative journeys characters undergo. By employing these advanced techniques, memoirists can create rich, nuanced portraits that resonate deeply with readers, making their stories not just read but felt and remembered.

MASTERING NON-LINEAR NARRATIVES

Non-linear narratives in memoir writing offer a unique and compelling way to tell a story. Unlike traditional linear narratives that follow a chronological order, non-linear narratives jump between different time periods, events, or perspectives. This structure can create a more dynamic and engaging reading experience, allowing the author to highlight connections, themes, and contrasts that might not be apparent in a straightforward chronological account. Mastering the non-linear narrative requires careful planning, a clear understanding of the story's overarching themes, and skillful writing to ensure clarity and coherence for the reader.

Conceptualizing the Non-Linear Structure

The first step in crafting a non-linear narrative is conceptualizing how the story will be structured. This involves deciding what parts of the story will be told out of chronological order and how these parts will intersect and interact. Authors should consider how jumping between different times or perspectives will enhance the story and contribute to its thematic development. The non-linear structure should serve a purpose, whether it's to create suspense, develop themes, or reveal character insights in a more impactful way.

Creating Coherence and Flow

One of the challenges of non-linear narratives is maintaining coherence and flow. Without the traditional chronological structure to guide them, readers might find it difficult to follow the story. To mitigate this, clear markers of time and place are essential. These can be explicit, like dates and locations at the beginning of chapters or sections, or more subtle, like distinct narrative voices or styles that differentiate the various timelines or perspectives.

Memoirists should also ensure that transitions between different parts of the narrative are smooth and logical. Each jump in time or perspective should feel natural and contribute to the overall story. The key is to guide the reader through the narrative in a way that is engaging and not disorienting.

Emphasizing Themes and Connections

Non-linear narratives are particularly effective in emphasizing themes and drawing connections between different events or periods in a person's life. By juxtaposing events from different times, memoirists can highlight patterns, contrasts, and recurring themes in their stories. This can create a deeper understanding of the memoir's central ideas and the author's experiences.

Balancing Mystery and Clarity

Non-linear narratives often create a sense of mystery, as the full story is revealed gradually and out of order. While this can be engaging, memoirists need to balance mystery with clarity. Readers should feel intrigued, not confused. Providing enough information to keep readers oriented, while withholding enough to maintain suspense, is a delicate balancing act.

Revisiting and Reinterpreting Events

Another advantage of non-linear narratives is the opportunity to revisit and reinterpret events from different perspectives or at different points in time. This can provide a more layered and nuanced understanding of the events and their impact on the memoirist's life.

Crafting a Satisfying Conclusion

In a non-linear narrative, the conclusion must bring together the various threads of the story in a satisfying way. It should provide a sense of closure, even if the story is told out of order. The conclusion is an opportunity to reflect on the journey, highlight the key insights gained, and underscore the memoir's overarching themes.

Mastering non-linear narratives in memoir writing allows authors to tell their stories in a dynamic and engaging way. It offers the flexibility to explore themes, characters, and events from multiple angles and timeframes, creating a rich and complex narrative tapestry. With careful planning, a focus on coherence, and skillful execution, non-linear narratives can transform a memoir into an immersive and thought-provoking reading experience.

THE USE OF SYMBOLISM AND METAPHOR

In memoir writing, the use of symbolism and metaphor can enrich the narrative, adding layers of meaning and depth. These literary devices allow authors to convey complex ideas, emotions, and themes in a more nuanced and impactful way. Symbolism involves using objects, events, or characters to represent something else, often abstract concepts or themes. Metaphors, on the other hand, involve direct comparisons between unrelated things, suggesting a similarity between them. Both can transform a memoir from a straightforward recounting of events into a more poetic, reflective, and profound narrative.

Enhancing Emotional Depth and Insight

Symbolism and metaphor can convey the emotional depth and insights of the memoirist in a way that direct descriptions may not. For instance, a long, arduous journey can be a powerful metaphor for personal growth and transformation. Similarly, an object like a family heirloom could symbolize heritage, memory, or loss. These devices allow readers to engage with the narrative on a deeper level, connecting with the underlying emotions and themes.

Creating Universal Resonance

By transcending the literal and the specific, symbolism and metaphor can make a memoir resonate more universally. They allow readers to find their own meanings and connections within the narrative, based on their experiences and interpretations. This not only makes the memoir more relatable but also invites a more active engagement from the reader, as they decipher and contemplate the deeper meanings.

Reflecting the Inner Journey

In memoirs, the journey is often as much internal as it is external. Symbolism and metaphor can effectively reflect this inner journey, providing a window into the memoirist's mind and heart. They can represent the author's evolving understanding of themselves, their relationships, and the world around them. For example, changing seasons can metaphorically represent stages of life, each with its unique challenges and beauty.

Crafting Rich and Layered Narratives

Symbolism and metaphor contribute to the richness and layer of the narrative. They add a poetic quality to the memoir, making the prose more evocative and vivid. This can transform ordinary events and experiences into something more significant and profound, elevating the narrative beyond the mundane.

Choosing Appropriate Symbols and Metaphors

Selecting the right symbols and metaphors is crucial. They should be relevant to the memoir's themes and resonate with the narrative. Overuse or inappropriate use of these devices can make the narrative confusing or heavy-handed. When used judiciously, they should seamlessly integrate into the narrative, enhancing rather than overwhelming the story.

Balancing Clarity with Complexity

While symbolism and metaphor add complexity to the narrative, memoirists must balance this with clarity. The primary goal is to communicate effectively with the reader, not to obscure the meaning. Memoirists should ensure that their use of these devices enriches the narrative without making it inaccessible or overly abstract.

Incorporating symbolism and metaphor in memoir writing offers a powerful way to deepen the narrative, making it more reflective, insightful, and engaging. These devices enable memoirists to communicate complex emotions and ideas subtly and creatively, enhancing the reader's experience and understanding of the story. By skillfully weaving symbolism and metaphor into their narratives, memoirists can create memoirs that are not only accounts of their lives but also works of art that resonate with readers on multiple levels.

PART IX: PERSONAL AND CULTURAL INFLUENCES

Writing About Trauma with Sensitivity

Writing about personal trauma in a memoir is a delicate endeavor that requires sensitivity, introspection, and a deep sense of responsibility. Traumatic experiences, whether they involve physical, emotional, or psychological challenges, are deeply personal and often painful to revisit. Yet, sharing these experiences can be therapeutic for the writer and impactful for the reader. It can foster understanding, empathy, and awareness about issues that are often shrouded in silence. However, the process of writing about trauma must be approached with care to avoid re-traumatization and to respect the sensitivity of the subject matter.

Navigating Personal Vulnerability

When delving into traumatic experiences, memoirists confront their vulnerabilities. It's essential to gauge one's emotional readiness to recount these experiences. Writing about trauma requires revisiting painful memories, which can be retraumatizing. Authors should consider their emotional state and seek support, whether through therapy, support groups, or trusted individuals, to ensure they are in a position to handle the emotional rigors of writing about trauma.

Honoring the Truth of the Experience

In writing about trauma, honoring the truth of the experience is paramount. This doesn't necessarily mean an exhaustive recounting of every detail but rather being true to the emotional reality of the experience. The focus should be on expressing the impact of the trauma and the journey of coping and healing. Authenticity in portraying traumatic experiences helps in validating the pain and resilience, not only of the writer but also of others who have faced similar challenges.

Balancing Detail with Discretion

Deciding how much detail to include is a critical consideration. Graphic descriptions of traumatic events can be distressing for both the writer and the reader. The aim should be to convey the gravity of the experience without delving into gratuitous details. Striking this balance is key to writing about trauma with respect and sensitivity.

The Therapeutic Potential of Writing

Writing about trauma can have therapeutic benefits. It allows for processing and making sense of what happened, providing a form of catharsis. It can also be empowering, as it involves reclaiming the narrative of one's own life. However, memoirists should be mindful that writing is not a substitute for professional therapy, and complex traumas often require additional support.

Impact on Readers

Considering the impact on readers is crucial when writing about trauma. Trigger warnings or content notices can be important to prepare readers for potentially distressing content. These warnings show consideration for the reader's wellbeing and provide them with the choice to engage with the material in a way that is safe for them.

Ethical Considerations

Writing about trauma also raises ethical considerations, especially when others are involved. It's important to respect the privacy and dignity of all individuals mentioned. In some cases, anonymizing details or seeking permission from those involved might be necessary. The memoirist must navigate the delicate balance between honesty and respect for the experiences and boundaries of others.

Reflecting on Healing and Growth

While the recounting of trauma is important, focusing on healing and growth can provide a hopeful perspective.

Highlighting the journey towards recovery, the lessons learned, and the strength gained can be inspiring. It shows that the memoir is not just about trauma but also about resilience, healing, and the capacity to rebuild.

Writing about trauma in a memoir is a profound and often challenging journey. It involves not only a deep exploration of one's past but also a careful consideration of how to present such experiences. By approaching this task with sensitivity, mindfulness, and a commitment to authenticity, memoirists can share their stories in a way that is healing, empowering, and resonant with readers. The memoir becomes a testament to the strength of the human spirit to overcome adversity and a source of solace and inspiration for those who may be facing similar struggles.

THE INTERSECTION OF MEMOIR AND CULTURAL COMMENTARY

Memoir writing, while deeply personal, often intersects with broader cultural and societal commentary. This intersection allows memoirists to extend their narratives beyond their own experiences, connecting their stories to larger themes that resonate within the broader social context. The memoir becomes a lens through which readers can explore and understand cultural, social, and historical realities. The integration of personal narrative with cultural commentary enriches the memoir, making it a powerful medium for reflection and discussion about the world in which we live.

Personal Stories as Reflectors of Societal Issues

Memoirs can be a reflection of the times and societies in which they are written. The personal stories and experiences narrated often mirror larger societal issues, such as social justice, inequality, cultural identity, and political turmoil. By sharing their personal journeys, memoirists can shed light on these broader issues, offering insights into how they affect individuals and communities.

The Role of the Memoirist as a Cultural Observer

Memoirists often take on the role of cultural observers. Their unique perspective, informed by their personal experiences, allows them to comment on cultural norms, societal changes, and historical events. This commentary can provide readers with a nuanced understanding of the complexities and intricacies of the cultural landscape. The memoirist's introspection and reflection can reveal the interconnectedness of personal experiences with wider cultural narratives.

Balancing Personal Narrative with Broader Commentary

One of the challenges in integrating cultural commentary into a memoir is maintaining a balance between the personal narrative and the broader societal context. The memoir should remain grounded in the author's personal experiences while using these experiences as a gateway to discuss larger themes. The key is to weave cultural commentary seamlessly into the narrative, ensuring that it complements rather than overshadows the personal story.

The Impact of Cultural Commentary in Memoirs

The inclusion of cultural commentary in memoirs can have a profound impact on readers. It can challenge perceptions, provoke thought, and inspire change. For some readers, it provides a new perspective on familiar issues; for others, it can be an eye-opening introduction to topics they are unfamiliar with. The memoirist's personal lens can make complex or abstract issues more relatable and understandable.

Addressing Contemporary Issues

Many memoirs address contemporary issues, providing a timely commentary on current events and trends. This relevance can make the memoir a powerful tool for engaging with the present moment, offering a space for readers to reflect on how these issues impact their lives and communities.

Reflecting on Historical and Cultural Context

Memoirs can also provide historical and cultural context, helping readers understand how past events and cultural shifts have shaped the present. By situating their personal stories within a historical framework, memoirists can contribute to a broader understanding of history and culture.

The Educational Value of Cultural Commentary

Incorporating cultural commentary into memoirs has an educational value. It can introduce readers to different cultures, histories, and societal structures, broadening their knowledge and perspective. This educational aspect can make memoirs a valuable resource for understanding and appreciating the diversity of human experiences.

The intersection of memoir and cultural commentary enhances the depth and breadth of the narrative. It transforms the memoir from a purely personal account into a multifaceted exploration of society, culture, and history. This blending of the personal with the cultural enriches the reader's experience, making memoirs not only a journey through an individual's life but also a journey through the wider world they inhabit. Through their stories, memoirists can offer powerful insights into the human condition, encouraging empathy, understanding, and reflection among their readers.

CRAFTING A UNIQUE AUTHORIAL PRESENCE

Creating a unique authorial presence in memoir writing is about establishing a distinct voice and perspective that resonates through the narrative, setting it apart from others. This presence is the memoirist's signature, a combination of their writing style, tone, perspective, and the personal insights they bring to their story. It's what makes a memoir not just a recounting of events, but a reflection of the individual behind the words. A strong authorial presence invites readers into the writer's world, offering them a unique lens through which to view the story being told.

Developing a Distinctive Voice

The voice in a memoir is pivotal. It should reflect the author's personality, experiences, and worldview. This voice can be shaped by various factors, including the author's background, the cultural and social contexts they come from, and their unique way of seeing the world. Developing this voice involves a deep understanding of oneself and how one wishes to be perceived by readers. It can be conversational, formal, humorous, reflective, or a mix of these qualities, depending on the story being told and the impact the author wants to have.

Infusing Personality into the Narrative

A memoir should be infused with the author's personality. This can be achieved through the choice of stories told, the perspectives shared, and the emotional tone of the writing. Whether it's through humor, candor, vulnerability, or wit, the author's personality should shine through, providing readers with a sense of who the author is as a person, not just as a narrator of events.

Balancing Personal Insights with Universal Themes

While a memoir is a deeply personal work, it should also touch on universal themes and experiences. A unique authorial presence comes from the ability to connect personal stories with broader human experiences. This involves exploring how personal anecdotes and reflections resonate with larger, more universal truths, making the memoir relatable to a wider audience.

Reflecting on the Writing Process

Reflecting on the writing process itself can also contribute to a unique authorial presence. By sharing their experiences, challenges, and revelations during the writing of the memoir, authors can provide readers with insights into their creative process. This metanarrative aspect can add an additional layer of depth to the memoir, making it a story not just about the events recounted, but also about the journey of writing them.

Evolving Presence Through the Memoir

An authorial presence may evolve throughout the memoir,

reflecting the author's journey. As the narrative progresses, changes in the author's perspective, understanding, or emotional state can be reflected in their writing style and tone. This evolution can add a dynamic quality to the memoir, engaging readers in the author's journey of growth and change.

Honesty and Authenticity

At the heart of a unique authorial presence is honesty and authenticity. Readers are often drawn to memoirs for their authentic portrayal of life experiences. Being honest, both about the events of the story and the author's feelings and reactions to them, is crucial. This authenticity is what helps forge a connection between the author and the reader, making the memoir a compelling and genuine reflection of the author's life.

Crafting a unique authorial presence in memoir writing is a process of introspection and expression. It involves finding one's voice, infusing the narrative with personality, and connecting personal experiences with universal themes. Through this process, memoirists can create a work that is not only a recounting of their life but also a reflection of their essence as a writer and as an individual. This unique presence engages readers, inviting them into the author's world and offering them a distinct perspective on the experiences shared within the pages of the memoir.

PART X: MORE ADVANCED TECHNIQUES AND REFLECTIONS

Advanced Pacing Strategies

Pacing in memoir writing is not just about the speed at which events unfold, but also about managing the emotional and psychological rhythm of the narrative. Advanced pacing strategies involve a nuanced understanding of how to guide the reader through the memoir, creating a journey that is as engaging and thought-provoking as it is emotionally resonant. These strategies include varying the pace to match the narrative's needs, using time as a structural element, and understanding the psychological impact of pacing on the reader.

Varying Pace for Narrative Effect

One effective strategy is to vary the pace throughout the memoir. Fast-paced sections can create a sense of urgency or excitement, propelling the narrative forward. Slower-paced sections, on the other hand, allow for deeper reflection and exploration of complex emotions or ideas. By varying the pace, memoirists can keep readers engaged and prevent the narrative from becoming monotonous.

- **Action vs. Reflection**: Balancing sections of action with periods of reflection is a key aspect of pacing. Action-driven scenes can provide momentum, while reflective passages can offer insight into the author's inner world and the significance of the events being recounted.

- **Short vs. Long Sections**: The length of sections or chapters can also affect pacing. Short, concise sections can speed up the narrative, while longer, more detailed sections can slow it down. Choosing the appropriate length for each section is crucial in maintaining the desired pace.

Using Time as a Structural Tool

Time can be a powerful tool in pacing. Flashbacks, flash-forwards, and non-linear timelines can add layers to the narrative, revealing information at strategically chosen moments. This can create suspense and keep readers intrigued, as they are gradually given the pieces of the story.

- **Managing Transitions**: When using non-linear

timelines, managing transitions between different times is crucial. Clear and smooth transitions help maintain the flow of the narrative and prevent confusion.

- **Revealing Information Gradually**: Withholding certain information and revealing it at key moments can be an effective pacing strategy. This gradual revelation keeps readers invested in the story, as they anticipate learning more.

Psychological Impact of Pacing

The pacing of a memoir can significantly impact the reader's psychological experience. A well-paced narrative can evoke a range of emotions, creating a journey that is emotionally fulfilling.

- **Building and Releasing Tension**: Pacing can be used to build and release tension. This emotional ebb and flow can mirror the memoirist's own experiences, drawing readers deeper into the story.
- **Creating Space for Empathy**: Slower-paced sections can create space for empathy, allowing readers to fully absorb and reflect on the more emotional or complex aspects of the memoir.
- **Enhancing Thematic Depth**: The pace at which themes are explored can affect their impact. Gradually delving into themes can allow for a more nuanced exploration, while a quicker pace can highlight more immediate or urgent themes.

Advanced pacing strategies in memoir writing require a delicate balance between moving the story forward and allowing space for reflection and emotional depth. By skillfully managing the pace, memoirists can create a narrative that is not only compelling in its storytelling but also profound in its emotional and psychological impact. This mastery of pacing ensures that the memoir remains engaging throughout, taking readers on a journey that is as varied and complex as life itself.

THE BLENDING OF GENRES IN MEMOIRS

In contemporary memoir writing, there is a growing trend towards blending different genres. This creative approach allows memoirists to expand the traditional boundaries of the genre, incorporating elements of fiction, poetry, historical narrative, and even speculative writing. This fusion creates a rich, multifaceted tapestry that can deepen the reader's engagement with the memoir, providing new ways of understanding the author's experiences and perspectives.

Expanding Beyond Traditional Memoir Boundaries

The blending of genres in memoirs reflects a broader trend in literature towards hybrid forms. This approach recognizes that life stories are complex and multifaceted, and sometimes cannot be adequately captured by traditional memoir conventions alone. By integrating different genres, memoirists can more effectively convey the nuances and complexities of their experiences.

Fictional Techniques in Memoirs

Incorporating fictional techniques, such as character development, plot construction, and dialogue, can enhance the narrative quality of a memoir. This doesn't mean altering the truth but rather using storytelling techniques to make the real-life events more engaging and relatable. For instance, reconstructing dialogue from memory, while staying true to the essence of conversations, can bring scenes to life in a way that pure exposition cannot.

Incorporating Poetic Elements

The use of poetic language and structure can imbue a memoir with lyrical quality, enhancing its emotional depth and resonance. Poetry allows for the expression of complex emotions and ideas in a condensed and powerful form. Memoirists might use poetic techniques such as metaphor, rhythm, and imagery to convey the intensity and profundity of their experiences.

Historical and Speculative Elements

Some memoirists weave in historical narratives, providing context and background to their personal stories. This can be particularly effective in memoirs that deal with significant historical events or cultural shifts. Additionally, speculative elements, such as imagining 'what could have been,' can offer a unique perspective on the author's experiences, exploring alternative realities and the impact of choices not made.

Balancing Authenticity with Creativity

While blending genres can enhance a memoir, it's crucial to balance creativity with authenticity. The heart of a memoir is its truthfulness. Any creative liberties taken should serve to deepen the reader's understanding and connection to the real-life experiences and emotions of the author, not detract from them.

Reflecting the Complexity of Memory and Experience

Using multiple genres can also reflect the complexity of memory and experience. Memory is often non-linear, fragmented, and influenced by emotions and subjective perceptions. A blended-genre approach can mirror this complexity, providing a more authentic representation of how the author perceives and remembers their life.

Challenges and Rewards

Blending genres in memoir writing presents both challenges and rewards. It requires skill and creativity to combine different elements seamlessly. However, when done effectively, it can result in a powerful and innovative narrative that pushes the boundaries of the genre, offering readers new insights into the human experience.

The blending of genres in memoirs is a testament to the evolving nature of storytelling. It reflects an understanding that life stories are varied and complex, often requiring a combination of narrative techniques to capture fully. This innovative approach not only enriches the memoir genre but also expands the ways in which we tell and understand personal narratives, inviting readers to engage with memoirs in new and exciting ways.

THE ROLE OF INTROSPECTION AND SELF-ANALYSIS

In memoir writing, introspection and self-analysis are vital components that offer depth and authenticity to the narrative. These processes involve the memoirist delving into their inner world, examining thoughts, feelings, motivations, and reactions to various life experiences. This introspective journey is not just about recounting events but about exploring and understanding the emotional and psychological landscapes that those events have shaped. By engaging in self-analysis, memoirists can provide readers with a deeper, more nuanced understanding of their life story, turning the memoir into a reflective and insightful exploration of the self.

Exploring the Inner Landscape

Introspection in memoir writing is akin to a deep dive into one's inner landscape. It involves examining personal beliefs, values, and emotional responses. Memoirists look back at their experiences and introspect on how these events have influenced their identity, worldview, and emotional makeup. This process can be both enlightening and challenging, as it often requires facing uncomfortable truths and unresolved emotions.

The Process of Self-Analysis

Self-analysis goes hand in hand with introspection. It involves dissecting and analyzing one's thoughts and behaviors, understanding the 'whys' behind actions and reactions. This can include exploring past traumas, unearthing subconscious motivations, and confronting personal flaws and contradictions. Through self-analysis, memoirists can offer readers a candid, often vulnerable insight into their journey of self-discovery and personal growth.

The Therapeutic Aspect of Introspection

For many memoirists, the process of introspection and self-analysis can be therapeutic. It provides a means to process and make sense of past experiences, to find closure, or to glean lessons from life's challenges and triumphs. This therapeutic aspect is not just limited to the memoirist; readers too can find solace, inspiration, and a sense of connection through the author's introspective journey.

Achieving Balance in the Narrative

While introspection and self-analysis are crucial, achieving balance in the narrative is important. The memoir should not become overly introspective to the point where it alienates the reader. Balancing inward reflection with outward narrative progression ensures the memoir remains engaging and relatable. It's about connecting the personal insights to a broader, more universal context.

Honesty and Vulnerability in Self-Analysis

Honesty and vulnerability are key in introspective and self-analytical writing. Being honest about one's flaws, mistakes, and lessons learned lends authenticity to the narrative. This honesty creates a bond of trust with the reader and adds to the memoir's emotional impact. Vulnerability, in revealing one's innermost thoughts and feelings, can be powerful, resonating deeply with readers and often providing them with insights into their own lives.

Reflecting on Change and Growth

An important aspect of introspection and self-analysis in memoirs is reflecting on change and growth. Memoirists often chart their evolution over time, showing how they have changed as a result of their experiences. This reflection not only highlights the memoir's narrative arc but also underscores the transformative power of life experiences.

Introspection and self-analysis in memoir writing turn the narrative into a meaningful exploration of the self. This introspective journey allows memoirists to delve deeply into their experiences, offering readers not just a recounting of life events, but a profound, reflective journey into the human psyche. By sharing their inner world with honesty and vulnerability, memoirists can create a narrative that is both deeply personal and universally resonant, offering insights and reflections that extend far beyond the pages of their memoir.

UNCONVENTIONAL FORMATS AND STRUCTURES

In memoir writing, experimenting with unconventional formats and structures can offer fresh perspectives and new ways of engaging with the narrative. Moving away from traditional linear storytelling, memoirists have the freedom to explore creative and innovative structures that can more accurately reflect the complexities of their experiences and memories. These unconventional approaches can challenge the reader's expectations and provide a unique reading experience, further enriching the memoir genre.

Experimenting with Format

The format of a memoir can significantly influence how the story is perceived and experienced by the reader. Memoirists might choose to structure their work in a variety of creative formats:

- **Epistolary Format**: Using letters, emails, or diary entries to tell the story. This format can provide an intimate glimpse into the author's thoughts and feelings over time.
- **Fragmented Narrative**: Presenting the memoir in

fragments or vignettes that are not chronologically ordered. This can mirror the way memories are often recalled and can create a sense of spontaneity and realism.

- **Mixed Media**: Incorporating photographs, drawings, documents, or even links to music and videos. This multimedia approach can enhance the narrative and provide a multi-sensory experience.

Structural Innovations

The structure of a memoir can also be used creatively to enhance the storytelling:

- **Circular or Non-Linear Structures**: Instead of a straight chronological progression, using a circular or non-linear structure can reflect the cyclical nature of life and memory.
- **Interwoven Timelines**: Alternating between different time periods or aspects of the author's life to create a tapestry of experiences that gradually builds a complete picture.
- **Thematic Organization**: Organizing the memoir around specific themes or motifs rather than chronology. This can allow for a deeper exploration of particular ideas or experiences.

The Role of Pacing in Unconventional Structures

In unconventional memoirs, pacing becomes crucial. The memoirist must carefully consider how the story unfolds in these non-traditional formats, ensuring that the narrative maintains momentum and keeps the reader engaged.

This might involve strategically placing certain stories or information to create suspense or develop themes gradually.

Balancing Innovation with Accessibility

While experimentation can be exciting, memoirists must also consider the accessibility of their work. Unconventional formats and structures should not be so complex or obscure that they alienate readers. The challenge is to find a balance between innovation and clarity, ensuring that the memoir remains engaging and comprehensible.

Reflecting the Subjective Nature of Memory

Unconventional structures can effectively reflect the subjective and often fragmented nature of memory. Memories are not always recalled in a linear fashion; they often come in flashes, out of order, and influenced by emotions. Using creative structures can authentically represent this aspect of human experience.

Enhancing the Memoir's Emotional Impact

Creative formats and structures can also enhance the emotional impact of the memoir. They can create a sense of immediacy, intimacy, or disorientation, mirroring the author's emotional journey. This can make the memoir more immersive and emotionally resonant.

Unconventional formats and structures in memoir writing allow authors to break free from traditional constraints and explore new ways of storytelling. By experimenting with different ways of presenting their stories, memoirists can create works that are not only reflective of their unique experiences but also contribute to the evolution of the memoir genre. These innovative approaches can offer readers new insights into the complexities of memory, identity, and the human experience, making each memoir a distinct and memorable journey.

THE ART OF SUBTEXT IN MEMOIRS

The use of subtext in memoir writing is a sophisticated technique that adds depth and complexity to the narrative. Subtext refers to the underlying themes, messages, or emotions that are not explicitly stated but are implied and felt throughout the memoir. It's the unspoken or less obvious aspect of the story that resonates with readers, often leaving a lasting impact. Mastering the art of subtext involves understanding how to convey more with less, allowing readers to read between the lines and engage with the memoir on a deeper level.

Conveying Depth Through Implication

Subtext works on the principle of implication. Instead of directly stating every emotion, thought, or theme, the memoirist implies them through descriptions, actions, dialogues, and even silences. This can involve showing how characters interact with each other or react in certain situations, revealing deeper truths about their relationships, thoughts, and feelings. For instance, a memoirist might describe a character's actions or body language in a way that subtly reveals their internal conflict or unspoken emotions.

Creating a Multidimensional Narrative

Subtext adds layers to the narrative, making it multidimensional. It invites readers to delve beneath the surface of the story, to explore the underlying themes and emotions that are not immediately apparent. This layering creates a richer reading experience, as the memoir is not just about the events that happened but also about what these events signify on a deeper, more symbolic level.

Engaging the Reader's Imagination and Interpretation

One of the powers of subtext is its ability to engage the reader's imagination and encourage personal interpretation. By not spelling everything out, subtext allows readers to draw their conclusions and meanings from the narrative. This active engagement can make the reading experience more personal and impactful, as readers connect their insights and experiences with the story being told.

Reflecting the Complexity of Human Experience

Subtext is an effective tool in capturing the complexity of human experience. Just as in real life, where much remains unsaid or is only indirectly expressed, subtext in memoirs can mirror this reality. It acknowledges that not everything is straightforward and that much of what shapes our lives lies beneath the surface.

Techniques for Creating Subtext

To create subtext, memoirists can use various techniques:

- **Symbolism**: Using symbols to represent larger themes or ideas.

- **Motifs**: Repeating certain images, words, or ideas to subtly reinforce themes.
- **Contrast and Irony**: Using contrast between what is said and what is meant, or between what is expected and what actually happens, to imply deeper meanings.
- **Selective Detailing**: Choosing specific details to focus on, ones that imply more than they describe outright.

Balancing Clarity with Ambiguity

While subtext enriches the memoir, balance is key. Too much ambiguity can leave readers confused, while too little can make the narrative too on-the-nose. Finding the right balance between clarity and ambiguity ensures that the memoir remains accessible but also thought-provoking.

The art of subtext in memoir writing is a nuanced and powerful tool. It enriches the narrative, providing depth and layers that invite readers to explore the story beyond its surface. By mastering subtext, memoirists can create a narrative that is not only engaging and insightful but also resonant with the complexities and subtleties of human life and relationships. This deeper engagement with the memoir allows readers to not just understand the author's story but also to reflect on their own experiences and interpretations, making the memoir a profound and resonant work.

ADVANCED TECHNIQUES IN DESCRIPTIVE WRITING

The mastery of descriptive writing is essential in memoirs, allowing the memoirist to vividly recreate scenes, emotions, and experiences for the reader. Advanced techniques in descriptive writing go beyond mere detailing of events; they involve evoking the senses, crafting vivid imagery, and creating an immersive experience for the reader. These techniques are crucial for transforming mere recollections into a rich tapestry of narrative that captivates and engages.

Evoking the Five Senses

To create a visceral experience, memoirists utilize language that evokes the five senses. Describing not just what was seen, but also the sounds, smells, tastes, and textures of an experience, brings a scene to life. This multisensory approach allows readers to fully immerse themselves in the narrative, experiencing the memoirist's world as vividly as if they were there.

The Art of Show, Don't Tell

'Show, don't tell' is a fundamental technique in descriptive writing. Instead of merely informing the reader about an event or emotion, memoirists show it through detailed description, action, dialogue, and thought. This technique helps to create a stronger emotional connection with the reader, as they are not just being told how to feel, but are experiencing the emotions themselves through the narrative.

Utilizing Figurative Language

Figurative language, including metaphors, similes, and personification, adds depth and creativity to descriptions. These elements of figurative language can transform ordinary descriptions into evocative and poetic passages, enriching the reader's experience. For instance, comparing a moment of despair to a storm not only describes the situation but also conveys its intensity and emotional impact.

Crafting Vivid Imagery

Vivid imagery is at the heart of effective descriptive writing. It involves creating detailed and specific descriptions that paint a clear picture in the reader's mind. The use of vivid imagery enables the memoirist to transport readers to different times and places, making the narrative more engaging and relatable.

Balancing Description with Narrative Pace

While rich descriptions are important, balancing them with narrative pace ensures that the memoir remains engaging and dynamic. Overly lengthy descriptions can slow down the narrative, while sparse descriptions might fail to convey the full experience. Finding the right balance keeps the reader invested in the story, maintaining a flow that feels natural and compelling.

Reflecting Emotional and Psychological Landscapes

Descriptive writing in memoirs also involves reflecting the emotional and psychological landscapes of the memoirist. Descriptions of settings, events, and characters are often imbued with emotional significance, reflecting the memoirist's inner world. This approach can provide deeper insights into the memoirist's experiences and perspectives.

Integrating Descriptions with Themes

Effective descriptive writing also involves integrating descriptions with the overall themes of the memoir. Descriptions can be used to reinforce and echo the memoir's central themes, providing a cohesive and unified narrative. This integration ensures that the descriptions serve a purpose beyond mere depiction, contributing to the memoir's deeper meaning and impact.

Advanced techniques in descriptive writing are vital for memoirists aiming to create a rich, immersive narrative. By mastering these techniques, memoirists can transform their memories into vivid, engaging, and emotionally resonant stories. Descriptive writing, when skillfully executed, not only depicts the memoirist's world but also invites the reader to step into it, experiencing the journey as their own.

PART XI: ADDING GREATER DEPTH TO YOUR MEMOIR

Crafting a Compelling Narrative Arc

In memoir writing, the narrative arc is not merely a chronological recounting of events, but a carefully structured journey that captivates and engages the reader. It's a blend of storytelling artistry, emotional depth, and introspective insight, woven together to create a narrative that resonates with authenticity and impact. The narrative arc in a memoir is about how the memoirist chooses to unfold their story, the pivotal moments they highlight, the conflicts they navigate, and the transformations they undergo.

The Memoir's Opening and Introduction of Conflict

A memoir typically begins by setting the stage for the reader, introducing them to the world of the memoirist. This includes providing context about the time, place, and significant people in the memoirist's life. Early on, the memoirist introduces the central conflict or question that propels the narrative. This conflict could be an external event that disrupts the memoirist's life or an internal struggle that they grapple with throughout the narrative.

Developing Tension and Deepening the Story

As the memoir progresses, the narrative arc deepens through the development of conflicts, challenges, and the unfolding of key events. This section is where the memoirist explores their struggles, confronts obstacles, and navigates complex emotions and relationships. The development phase is integral in building tension and adding layers to the narrative, as it provides insights into the memoirist's journey and the transformations they experience.

Climactic Moments and Turning Points

The climax in a memoir is the moment of highest tension and drama. It is the turning point where the memoirist confronts the central conflict head-on. This could manifest as a pivotal event, a significant realization, or a moment of profound change. The climax is often where the memoirist faces their deepest fears, makes critical decisions, or undergoes a significant transformation.

Navigating Resolution and Change

In the latter part of the memoir, the narrative moves towards resolving the conflicts introduced earlier. This doesn't necessarily mean a conventional resolution but rather a point where the memoirist finds some understanding, acceptance, or peace regarding the central conflict. It often involves a reflection on how the experiences have shaped the memoirist, highlighting their growth, learning, and changes.

The Role of Reflection in the Narrative Arc

Reflection is a critical aspect of the narrative arc in a memoir. Throughout the narrative, the memoirist engages in introspection, examining their actions, thoughts, and the implications of their experiences. This reflective aspect adds depth to the narrative, allowing readers to connect with the memoirist's internal journey and the wisdom gleaned from their experiences.

Weaving in Themes and Insights

Throughout the narrative arc, the memoirist weaves in various themes and insights that emerge from their story. These could be lessons learned, truths uncovered, or realizations about themselves and the world. The integration of these themes adds richness to the memoir, making it more than just a personal story, but a reflection of broader human experiences and truths.

The Unfolding Journey

The narrative arc in a memoir is essentially the unfolding of the memoirist's journey. It captures the essence of their experiences, the conflicts they navigate, and the transformations they undergo. This journey is not just about the events that happen but also about the emotional and psychological journey that the memoirist undertakes.

Crafting a compelling narrative arc in a memoir is about structuring the story in a way that engages and moves the reader. It involves more than just laying out the facts of the memoirist's life; it's about crafting a journey that is emotionally rich, introspectively deep, and narratively satisfying. The memoirist's skill in building this arc determines how effectively they can draw the reader into their world, share their experiences, and leave a lasting impact.

PSYCHOLOGICAL INSIGHTS IN CHARACTER DEVELOPMENT

In memoir writing, delving into the psychological insights of characters, including the memoirist, enriches the narrative and adds a layer of depth to the storytelling. Understanding and portraying the psychological dimensions of characters is not just about recounting actions or events but about exploring the motivations, emotions, and inner conflicts that drive those actions. This exploration offers a window into the complexities of human behavior and relationships, making the characters more relatable, authentic, and multidimensional.

Exploring Motivations and Emotions

The key to developing psychological depth in characters is to explore their motivations and emotions. What drives them? What fears or desires lie beneath their actions? Understanding these aspects allows memoirists to portray their characters, including themselves, in a more nuanced and empathetic way. It involves examining not just what the characters do, but why they do it, and how they feel about it.

The Memoirist's Self-Analysis

For the memoirist, self-analysis is a crucial part of this process. It involves introspection and honesty, a willingness to delve into personal strengths, weaknesses, fears, and desires. This self-analysis can be challenging, as it requires facing uncomfortable truths, but it's also what makes the memoir genuine and compelling. The memoirist's journey of self-discovery and understanding becomes a central element of the narrative.

Psychological Development Over Time

Another important aspect is showing the psychological development of characters over time. How do they change throughout the narrative? What lessons do they learn, and how do these lessons affect their behavior and perspective? This development can be a powerful reflection of the memoirist's growth and transformation.

The Impact of Relationships and Interactions

The psychological depth of characters is often revealed through their relationships and interactions with others. How characters relate to each other, how they communicate, and how they are affected by each other's actions can provide significant insights into their psychological makeup. These interactions can highlight conflicts, compatibilities, and the dynamics that shape their relationships.

Balancing Vulnerability with Respect

In writing about real people, memoirists must balance vulnerability with respect. While exploring the psychological aspects of characters, it's important to treat their stories with care and consideration. This is particularly crucial when dealing with sensitive or private aspects of their lives.

Reflections on the Human Condition

Through exploring the psychological insights of characters, memoirists can offer reflections on the human condition. They can delve into themes such as identity, resilience, love, loss, and redemption, connecting personal experiences with universal human experiences. This connection can make the memoir resonate with readers, offering them insights into their own lives.

The Use of Narrative Techniques

Narrative techniques such as inner monologues, flashbacks, and reflective passages can be effective in revealing the psychological depth of characters. These techniques allow memoirists to show what's going on inside the characters' minds, providing readers with a direct view of their thoughts and feelings.

Developing psychological insights in character development is a vital element of memoir writing. It transforms the narrative from a mere recounting of events into a deep exploration of the characters' inner worlds. This exploration enriches the memoir, making it a more powerful and emotionally engaging read. By offering these insights, memoirists not only tell their stories but also illuminate the complexities of human psychology, making their memoirs resonate with authenticity and depth.

THE USE OF LITERARY DEVICES IN MEMOIRS

Incorporating literary devices into memoirs elevates the narrative, offering a richer and more textured exploration of the memoirist's experiences and insights. These devices, ranging from metaphor and simile to imagery, symbolism, and irony, serve not merely as ornamental elements but as integral tools that enhance the storytelling. They imbue the narrative with depth, nuance, and emotional resonance, transforming the memoir from a mere recounting of events into an engaging literary experience.

Metaphors and Similes for Vivid Imagery

Metaphors and similes enrich the memoir's language, drawing comparisons that illuminate and deepen the reader's understanding. A metaphor might equate a life-changing decision to standing at a crossroads, while a simile could describe a period of joy as radiant as a sunlit day. These comparisons offer vivid imagery and enhance the emotional impact of the narrative.

Symbolism for Deeper Meaning

Symbolism in memoirs involves using objects, events, or characters to represent larger ideas or themes. A childhood home, for instance, might symbolize lost innocence or a longing for stability. Symbolism allows memoirists to convey complex themes and emotions subtly, adding layers of meaning to the narrative.

Irony for Reflective Insight

Irony in memoirs can offer reflective insights or highlight contradictions. It might manifest in the difference between what the memoirist hoped for in a situation and the actual outcome. Irony can introduce a critical perspective or add humor to the narrative, enriching the memoir's texture.

Flashbacks and Foreshadowing for Narrative Structure

Flashbacks allow memoirists to delve into their past, shedding light on how previous experiences have shaped their present. Foreshadowing hints at future events or revelations, creating suspense and keeping the reader engaged in the unfolding story.

Allusions for Contextual Depth

Allusions to literature, history, or culture can provide a contextual depth to the memoir, linking the memoirist's personal experiences to broader themes and universal issues. These references can resonate with informed readers, adding an intellectual layer to the narrative.

Crafting Authentic Dialogue

Dialogue in memoirs can bring characters and scenes to life, revealing personality traits and relationship dynamics. Effective dialogue contributes to character development and enhances the narrative's authenticity.

The Memoirist's Tone and Voice

The tone and voice in a memoir are crucial elements that reflect the memoirist's personality and perspective. The tone might vary from humorous to solemn, while the voice should remain authentic and distinctive, providing a unique lens through which the story is told.

Balancing Literary Elements

The memoirist must balance these literary elements to enhance the storytelling without overwhelming it. The use of literary devices should serve the narrative, providing clarity and depth, rather than complicating the story.

In memoir writing, literary devices play a crucial role in transforming personal experiences into compelling narratives. By skillfully employing these tools, memoirists can create a nuanced, emotionally resonant story that engages readers not just with the events of the memoir but with its deeper emotional and thematic undercurrents. These devices enrich the narrative, making the memoir a work of art that captivates and moves its audience.

PART XII: THE FUTURE, ETHICS AND PHILOSOPHY AND PURPOSE

Writing About the Future in Memoirs

In memoir writing, discussions about the future offer a unique dimension, contrasting past experiences with expectations, hopes, and uncertainties about what lies ahead. While memoirs are predominantly reflections on past events, incorporating future aspirations or contemplations can provide a dynamic perspective, connecting past experiences with future possibilities. This approach allows memoirists to explore the evolution of their dreams, goals, and how their past has shaped their outlook on the future.

Projecting Forward from Past Experiences

Memoirists often use their past experiences as a foundation for projecting into the future. This projection can be a powerful tool for illustrating how past events have influenced their aspirations and expectations. For instance, overcoming significant challenges in the past might lead to a sense of optimism and resilience about future endeavors. This forward-looking perspective can offer insights into the memoirist's growth and the lessons they carry into the future.

Exploring Aspirations and Dreams

Discussing future aspirations and dreams adds an aspirational quality to the memoir. It allows readers to see beyond the events recounted, providing a glimpse into the memoirist's hopes and ambitions. This exploration can serve as an inspiration to readers, showcasing the potential for growth and change regardless of past circumstances.

The Role of Uncertainty and Speculation

Addressing the future inevitably involves grappling with uncertainty and speculation. Memoirists might express their hopes, fears, and uncertainties about what lies ahead, reflecting on the unpredictable nature of life. This honest acknowledgment of uncertainty resonates with the universal human experience of facing an unknown future.

Linking the Past, Present, and Future

Memoirs that weave together past, present, and future create a narrative tapestry that captures the continuum of the memoirist's life. This linkage underscores the impact of past experiences on present circumstances and future prospects. It can highlight the enduring effects of certain events or decisions, demonstrating how the past continues to influence the present and future.

Reflecting on Change and Continuity

Memoirs provide an opportunity to reflect on change and continuity in life. By looking to the future, memoirists can ponder which aspects of their life or self have changed over time and which have remained constant. This reflection can offer profound insights into personal growth and the essence of the memoirist's identity.

The Impact of Time on Perspectives

Memoirs that incorporate future perspectives often reflect on how the passage of time affects one's outlook. The memoirist may contrast their former expectations of the future with their current aspirations, highlighting how perspectives can shift over time due to new experiences, knowledge, and personal growth.

Imagining Alternate Futures

Some memoirists engage in imagining alternate futures, considering how different choices or events might have led to different outcomes. This speculative approach can be a thought-provoking exploration of the role of choice and chance in shaping one's path.

The Influence of Hopes on Personal Narrative

Integrating future hopes and dreams into a memoir can significantly influence the overall narrative. It adds a forward-moving dynamic to the story, suggesting a trajectory that extends beyond the events recounted. This forward-looking perspective can infuse the memoir with a sense of purpose and direction, reinforcing the memoirist's ongoing journey.

Incorporating the future into memoir writing enriches the narrative, offering a more comprehensive view of the memoirist's life and experiences. By connecting past experiences with future aspirations and reflections, memoirists create a multi-dimensional narrative that not only recounts where they have been but also anticipates where they are going. This exploration of the future within the memoir adds depth to the understanding of the memoirist's life, presenting a holistic view that encompasses their past, present, and future.

ETHICAL DILEMMAS IN MEMOIR WRITING

Memoir writing often involves navigating ethical dilemmas, stemming from the need to balance truth-telling with the potential impact on the people featured in the narrative and the wider community. These dilemmas can range from concerns about privacy and consent to the responsibilities of representing truth and avoiding harm. Addressing these ethical challenges is crucial in memoir writing, as it not only affects the integrity of the memoirist but also the lives of those who are part of their story.

Balancing Truth and Privacy

One of the primary ethical dilemmas in memoir writing is balancing the memoirist's commitment to truth with the privacy rights of the individuals featured in their story. This balance is complex, especially when the narrative involves sensitive or potentially damaging information about others. The memoirist must navigate how to truthfully recount their experiences while respecting the privacy and dignity of others, which may involve altering identifying details, using pseudonyms, or selectively omitting certain aspects of the story.

Consent and Representation

Obtaining consent from people who are prominently featured in the memoir is an ethical consideration. While it's not always feasible or necessary to obtain explicit consent for every detail, memoirists often face the dilemma of how to fairly represent people's stories, especially in cases where their perspectives differ significantly from the memoirist's. This extends to how different groups and communities are portrayed, ensuring that the memoir does not inadvertently perpetuate stereotypes or misrepresentations.

Dealing with Family and Personal Relationships

Writing about family members and close personal relationships can be particularly ethically challenging. The memoirist must consider the impact their narrative may have on these relationships. The portrayal of family members and friends not only raises questions about privacy and consent but also about loyalty, betrayal, and the repercussions that come with revealing family secrets or personal conflicts.

The Responsibility of Honesty

Memoirists have a responsibility to be honest and authentic in their storytelling. However, they also need to acknowledge the subjective nature of memory and perception. The ethical dilemma arises in deciding how to present events and experiences that might be disputed or remembered differently by others. This involves a careful consideration of how memory, subjectivity, and factual accuracy intersect in the narrative.

The Impact on Communities

Memoirists also need to consider the impact of their story on the communities they represent. This is particularly important when the memoir touches on issues like race, ethnicity, gender, or cultural background. The memoirist holds the responsibility of ensuring that their personal story does not inadvertently harm or misrepresent the larger communities to which they belong.

Navigating Legal Implications

Legal considerations, such as libel and defamation, are also part of the ethical landscape in memoir writing. Memoirists must ensure that what they write about others is either demonstrably true or clearly presented as opinion to avoid legal repercussions, adding another layer to the ethical decision-making process.

Reflecting on the Purpose of the Memoir

Finally, memoirists face the ethical dilemma of reflecting on the purpose and intent of their memoir. This involves considering why they are telling their story and what they hope to achieve with it. Is it for healing, closure, to shed light on broader issues, or to settle scores? The underlying intent can significantly influence the ethical choices made in the writing process.

Navigating the ethical dilemmas in memoir writing is a nuanced and complex process. It requires a careful balance between honesty, artistic expression, and the ethical implications of telling a real-life story that involves real people. By thoughtfully addressing these dilemmas, memoirists can create narratives that are not only compelling and truthful but also respectful and sensitive to the lives and stories of others. This ethical mindfulness ensures that the memoir serves as a vehicle for understanding and connection, rather than conflict or harm.

THE INTERSECTION OF MEMOIR AND PHILOSOPHY

The intersection of memoir and philosophy presents a unique fusion where personal narratives delve into profound philosophical questioning and exploration. This blend allows memoirists to not only recount their life experiences but also to engage deeply with existential, ethical, and metaphysical questions. The philosophical dimension adds depth and breadth to the memoir, elevating it from a mere life story to a thoughtful exploration of the human condition.

Philosophical Themes in Personal Narratives

Memoirists often find themselves naturally exploring philosophical themes through their personal narratives. These themes can include the nature of identity, the concept of free will versus determinism, the search for meaning in life, and the contemplation of mortality. By intertwining these philosophical explorations with personal experiences, memoirists can offer unique insights into how such abstract concepts manifest in everyday life.

Existential Reflections

Many memoirs inherently contain existential reflections, where memoirists grapple with questions about the essence of existence, purpose, and the individual's place in the world. These reflections are often prompted by pivotal life experiences, such as facing a life-threatening illness, enduring loss, or undergoing significant life changes. The memoir becomes a space for the memoirist to ponder existential questions and share their journey towards understanding or acceptance.

Ethics and Morality in Personal Stories

Memoirs frequently touch on issues of ethics and morality, particularly when recounting personal dilemmas, conflicts, and decisions. Memoirists might reflect on their moral beliefs, the ethical implications of their choices, and the lessons learned from confronting moral challenges. This introspection can provide a nuanced perspective on how ethical considerations shape personal journeys.

The Influence of Philosophical Texts and Thinkers

Some memoirists draw directly from philosophical texts and thinkers, using them as a framework or reference point for their own experiences. References to philosophers like Sartre, Nietzsche, or Eastern philosophical traditions can enrich the narrative, providing a broader context for the memoirist's reflections and experiences. This incorporation of philosophy can also introduce readers to these concepts, making the memoir an educational journey into philosophical thought.

Contemplating Human Nature and Society

Memoirs often explore the nature of humanity and society,

delving into questions about social constructs, human behavior, and the dynamics of personal relationships within societal contexts. Memoirists might reflect on how societal norms and values have influenced their life choices and identity. This exploration can offer insightful commentary on the human condition and societal structures.

Philosophical Inquiry Through Personal Experience

The power of integrating philosophy into memoirs lies in the ability to explore philosophical questions through the lens of personal experience. Rather than abstract theorization, these inquiries are grounded in the lived experiences of the memoirist, making philosophical concepts more relatable and tangible for the reader.

The Search for Meaning

At the heart of many memoirs is the search for meaning – a fundamental philosophical pursuit. Memoirists often recount their efforts to find meaning in their experiences, whether through overcoming adversity, engaging in creative pursuits, or connecting with others. This search for meaning can resonate deeply with readers, who may be on their own quests for understanding and purpose.

The intersection of memoir and philosophy enriches the memoir genre, offering readers not just a window into the memoirist's life but also an invitation to engage with deeper philosophical questions. By weaving philosophical explorations into their narratives, memoirists create a rich tapestry of thought and experience. This fusion encourages readers to ponder their own beliefs, values, and the larger questions of life, making the memoir a catalyst for personal reflection and philosophical inquiry.

PART XIII: EVEN DEEPER – LAYERS THAT ENHANCE EMOTION

Advanced Dialogue Techniques

In memoir writing, dialogue is not just a tool for recounting conversations but a dynamic element that can reveal character, advance the plot, and deepen the emotional resonance of the narrative. Advanced dialogue techniques in memoirs involve crafting conversations that are not only authentic but also serve multiple functions within the narrative. Effective dialogue in a memoir can illuminate character traits, expose conflicts, convey subtext, and evoke the memoirist's world, making it a crucial aspect of the memoir's structure.

Crafting Authentic Dialogue

The authenticity of dialogue is paramount in memoir writing. It should reflect the way people speak in real life, capturing their unique voices, dialects, and speech patterns. Authentic dialogue helps to bring characters to life and adds realism to the narrative. However, memoirists often face the challenge of recalling exact conversations. In such cases, it's the essence or the emotional truth of the dialogue that matters more than word-for-word accuracy.

Revealing Character Through Dialogue

Dialogue is a powerful tool for character development. Through conversations, memoirists can reveal aspects of a character's personality, beliefs, and background without explicitly stating them. How a character speaks, what they say, and what they choose not to say can all provide insights into their character. For example, a character's choice of words can reveal their education level, cultural background, or emotional state.

Advancing the Narrative with Dialogue

Dialogue in memoirs can also serve to advance the narrative. It can be used to introduce new information, move the plot forward, or build tension. Skillful use of dialogue can propel the story without relying solely on narrative exposition. By revealing key information through conversations, memoirists can maintain the momentum of the narrative and keep readers engaged.

Conveying Subtext in Dialogue

Subtext in dialogue refers to the underlying messages or emotions that are not explicitly stated but are implied. Effective dialogue often contains subtext, where characters say one thing but mean another, or where their words carry a deeper emotional or thematic significance. This layer of subtext adds depth to the dialogue, engaging readers to read between the lines and understand the unspoken implications.

Reflecting the Era and Environment

Dialogue can also reflect the era and environment in which the memoir is set. The way people speak can evoke a particular time and place, immersing the reader in the memoirist's world. This might involve using period-specific slang, jargon, or references that anchor the memoir in its historical and cultural context.

Balancing Dialogue with Narrative

In memoir writing, balancing dialogue with narrative description is important. While dialogue can enliven the narrative, it needs to be integrated seamlessly with descriptive passages. This balance ensures that the memoir maintains its flow and coherence, with dialogue complementing rather than dominating the narrative.

Dialogue as a Reflection of Relationships

Dialogue in memoirs can also be used to explore and reveal the dynamics of relationships. How characters interact with each other in conversation can shed light on their relationships, conflicts, and emotional connections. For instance, the way family members speak to each other can reveal the nature of their bond, underlying tensions, or affection.

Crafting effective dialogue in memoirs requires a combination of authenticity, skillful character development, narrative advancement, and emotional depth. By employing advanced dialogue techniques, memoirists can create conversations that are not only believable but also multi-dimensional, contributing significantly to the development of characters, the progression of the narrative, and the overall impact of the memoir. Well-crafted dialogue enriches the memoir, providing readers with a more immersive and emotionally engaging experience.

THE CHALLENGE OF WRITING ABOUT HAPPINESS

Writing about happiness in memoirs presents a unique challenge. Often, narratives are driven by conflict, struggle, and overcoming adversity, as these elements generally make for a compelling story. However, capturing the essence of happiness, contentment, and joy in writing is equally important, as it provides a balanced portrayal of life's experiences. Exploring the nuances of happiness in a memoir requires a thoughtful approach, delving into what happiness means to the memoirist and how it has shaped their life.

Defining Personal Happiness

Happiness can mean different things to different people. For some, it might be found in moments of achievement or success, for others in quiet moments of contentment, and for others still in the joy of relationships and connections. Memoirists need to explore and define what happiness means to them personally. This exploration involves introspection and reflection on the moments and experiences that have brought them joy and fulfillment.

The Subtlety of Happy Moments

Unlike dramatic or traumatic events, moments of happiness can be subtle and fleeting, making them harder to capture in writing. These moments often lack the dramatic tension that characterizes more conflict-driven narratives. The challenge for memoirists is to convey the significance of these quieter moments of joy and how they have impacted their lives. This might involve focusing on sensory details, emotional reactions, or the context in which these moments occurred.

Happiness in Everyday Life

Memoirists can find rich material in the everyday moments of happiness. This includes the small, often overlooked experiences that bring joy, such as a conversation with a loved one, a peaceful walk, or a moment of laughter. By highlighting these everyday moments, memoirists can show how happiness is often found in the ordinary and mundane, offering readers a relatable and authentic perspective on joy.

Happiness Amidst Adversity

Another aspect to explore is finding happiness amidst adversity. Many memoirs include stories of overcoming challenges, and within these narratives, there are often moments of joy and triumph. Exploring how happiness coexists with struggle can add depth to the memoir, showing the complexity of human emotions and experiences.

Reflecting on the Sources of Happiness

Memoirists might also reflect on the sources of their happiness. This can include relationships, personal achievements, growth, spirituality, or a connection to nature. By examining these sources, memoirists can offer insights into what brings fulfillment and contentment in life.

The Impact of Happiness on Personal Growth

Happiness can significantly impact personal growth and perspective. Memoirists can explore how happy experiences have contributed to their development, shaped their values, or changed their outlook on life. This exploration can provide a counterpoint to the more challenging aspects of their story, offering a holistic view of their journey.

Connecting with Readers through Joy

Writing about happiness can create a connection with readers, as it taps into the universal pursuit of joy and fulfillment. By sharing their happy moments, memoirists can inspire and uplift readers, reminding them of the joyous possibilities in life.

Writing about happiness in memoirs, while challenging, is an essential aspect of portraying a full and authentic life story. It requires a thoughtful and introspective approach, focusing on the subtleties and complexities of joyful experiences. By capturing these moments, memoirists can offer a balanced narrative that reflects the full spectrum of human experience, connecting with readers through shared moments of happiness and joy.

THE ROLE OF RESEARCH IN DEEPENING YOUR MEMOIR

In memoir writing, research plays a crucial role in deepening the narrative, ensuring accuracy, and enriching the story with context and detail. While memoirs are based on personal experiences and memories, incorporating research can provide a broader perspective and add layers of depth to the narrative. This research can range from verifying dates and facts to exploring historical, cultural, or societal contexts relevant to the memoirist's story. Engaging in research enhances the memoir's authenticity and credibility and can provide new insights into the memoirist's experiences.

Verifying Facts and Events

One of the primary roles of research in memoir writing is to verify facts and events. Even with vivid memories, details can become blurred or altered over time. Researching specific dates, places, and events can help memoirists ensure the accuracy of their narrative. This might involve looking at old letters, diaries, photographs, or public records. Ensuring factual accuracy is essential for maintaining the memoir's credibility.

Exploring Historical and Cultural Context

Researching the historical and cultural context of the events recounted in the memoir can add significant depth to the narrative. Understanding the broader societal and historical backdrop against which personal stories unfold can provide readers with a more comprehensive view of the memoirist's experiences. This context can be particularly important in memoirs that touch on significant historical events, social movements, or cultural shifts.

Delving into Family History

For many memoirists, exploring family history is a crucial aspect of their research. This can involve tracing genealogies, uncovering family stories, and understanding the heritage and legacy passed down through generations. Researching family history can reveal surprising connections and patterns, adding richness and depth to the memoir.

Investigating Specific Themes or Topics

Memoirs often explore specific themes or topics deeply connected to the memoirist's experiences. Researching these topics can provide valuable insights and perspectives that enhance the narrative. For instance, a memoirist writing about their experience with a particular illness might research medical information, patient experiences, and treatment advancements. This research can lend authority to their narrative and help readers understand the topic more deeply.

Enriching Descriptions and Settings

Research can also be used to enrich descriptions and settings in the memoir. For memoirists writing about places or times distant from their current reality, research can help them recreate those settings authentically. This might involve researching geographical details, cultural norms, or the political climate of a particular era.

Integrating Interviews and Personal Accounts

In some memoirs, incorporating interviews or personal accounts from others who share a part of the memoirist's story can add diverse perspectives and dimensions. This research can provide alternative viewpoints and insights, enriching the narrative and providing a more rounded understanding of the events and experiences described.

Overcoming Memory Gaps

Research can be particularly valuable in overcoming gaps in memory. By researching events, places, or people connected to their story, memoirists can fill in the blanks in their recollections, providing a more complete and accurate account of their experiences.

Respecting Privacy and Ethical Considerations

In conducting research, especially when it involves other people, memoirists must navigate privacy and ethical considerations. This includes respecting the privacy of others when delving into shared histories and being mindful of how the inclusion of certain information might impact the people involved.

Engaging in research is a fundamental aspect of memoir

writing that goes beyond mere fact-checking. It involves immersing oneself in the exploration of contexts, histories, and perspectives that surround and infuse the memoirist's personal story. Through research, memoirists can deepen their narrative, providing readers with a richer, more engaging, and more informed account of their life experiences. This process not only enhances the memoir's authenticity but also opens new avenues for understanding and connecting with the memoirist's journey.

ADDRESSING GLOBAL ISSUES THROUGH PERSONAL STORIES

In memoir writing, addressing global issues through the lens of personal stories is a powerful way to connect individual experiences with larger societal and world events. This approach not only provides a human face to often abstract and complex issues but also highlights the interconnectedness of personal and global experiences. Memoirists who intertwine their personal narratives with broader global themes can offer unique insights into the impacts of these issues on individual lives, making their stories both intimate and universally relevant.

Personalizing Global Issues

When memoirists incorporate global issues into their narratives, they personalize these often broad and complex topics. Issues like climate change, migration, war, or global pandemics, which can seem distant or overwhelming, are brought down to a human scale. The memoirist's personal experiences with these issues offer readers a tangible and relatable perspective, making these global concerns more accessible and understandable.

Reflecting on the Impact of Societal Events

Memoirists often reflect on how larger societal events have impacted their lives. This reflection can include how political decisions, economic changes, or social movements have directly or indirectly influenced their personal journey. For example, a memoirist might write about how a recession affected their career path or how a social justice movement changed their personal beliefs and actions.

Providing a Window into Different Cultures and Experiences

Memoirs that address global issues can also provide readers with a window into different cultures and experiences. By sharing their stories, memoirists offer insights into how life in various parts of the world is affected by global events and issues. This can foster empathy and understanding among readers from different backgrounds, highlighting the shared human experiences amidst diverse cultural contexts.

The Role of the Memoirist as a Witness

In writing about global issues, the memoirist often takes on the role of a witness, sharing firsthand accounts of events or situations that readers may have only seen through the lens of media. This eyewitness perspective can offer a more nuanced and personal view of these events, adding depth and complexity to the public narrative.

Exploring the Interplay of Personal and Global

Memoirs that delve into global issues often explore the interplay between the personal and the global. Memoirists examine how their personal story is part of a larger narrative, reflecting on their role and responsibilities in a globally connected world. This exploration can challenge readers to consider their place in addressing global issues.

Challenging Stereotypes and Broadening Perspectives

Memoirs can also challenge stereotypes and broaden perspectives on global issues. By sharing personal experiences that defy common narratives or simplistic views, memoirists can contribute to a more nuanced understanding of complex issues. This can be particularly impactful in cases where the memoirist belongs to a group that is often misrepresented or misunderstood in the global discourse.

The Transformative Power of Storytelling

Storytelling has a transformative power, and memoirs that address global issues can contribute to this transformation. By sharing their personal stories, memoirists can inspire change, raise awareness, and encourage action on these issues. The personal narrative becomes a tool for advocacy and education, demonstrating the power of individual stories in contributing to global conversations.

Incorporating global issues into memoirs bridges the gap between the personal and the universal, offering readers a unique perspective on the world. Memoirists who tackle these issues through their personal narratives contribute to a deeper understanding of global events, cultures, and challenges. By weaving their personal experiences with larger global themes, memoirists can create narratives that are not only reflective of their own lives but also resonate with broader societal and global contexts. This approach enriches the memoir genre, turning personal stories into powerful reflections on the world and our place within it.

THE USE OF IRONY AND PARADOX IN MEMOIRS

Irony and paradox are literary devices that, when skillfully employed in memoirs, can significantly enhance the narrative's depth and complexity. Irony involves a contrast between expectations and reality, where the outcome is different from what was anticipated. Paradox, on the other hand, is a statement or situation that, despite apparently sound reasoning from acceptable premises, leads to a conclusion that seems logically unacceptable or self-contradictory. In the context of memoir writing, these devices can be used to reflect the complexities of life, offer insightful observations, and engage readers in a more profound understanding of the memoirist's experiences.

Irony as a Reflection of Life's Unpredictability

Irony in memoirs mirrors the unpredictability and complexities of life. It highlights the discrepancies between what we hope or plan and what actually happens. This can range from situational irony, where events turn out differently from what was expected, to dramatic irony, where the reader knows something the narrator only realizes later. For example, a memoirist might describe their younger self's aspirations or misconceptions with a sense of irony, reflecting on the naivety or innocence of those earlier beliefs compared to their current understanding.

The Use of Paradox in Conveying Complex Truths

Paradoxes in memoirs are powerful for conveying complex truths and the multifaceted nature of human experiences. They can illustrate how seemingly contradictory elements in life can coexist, such as finding freedom in confinement or experiencing joy in sorrow. These paradoxes encourage readers to think deeply and appreciate the nuances and contradictions inherent in life and human nature.

Irony in Character Development

Irony can be a tool for character development in memoirs. It can be used to reveal deeper truths about the memoirist or other characters, often highlighting flaws, misconceptions, or the irony of their actions versus their intentions. This utilization of irony adds layers to the characters, making them more relatable and human.

Paradoxical Situations and Insights

Memoirists often find themselves in paradoxical situations, which can be explored in their narratives. These situations can range from personal dilemmas to broader life circumstances that seem to contradict themselves. Exploring these paradoxes can offer insightful reflections and reveal deeper understandings of the memoirist's journey.

The Role of Irony in Memoir's Tone

The tone of a memoir can be significantly shaped by the use

of irony. A memoirist might adopt an ironic tone to discuss past events, providing a means to approach difficult or painful memories with a blend of detachment and insight. This tone can also introduce humor into the narrative, making the memoir more engaging for readers.

Using Paradox to Challenge Readers

Paradoxes in memoirs challenge readers to think critically and question their assumptions about life, relationships, and beliefs. By presenting readers with these contradictions, memoirists invite them to explore the complexities of life and consider different perspectives.

Irony as a Commentary on Social and Cultural Norms

Irony can also be used as a commentary on social and cultural norms. Memoirists might employ irony to critique societal expectations, cultural norms, or historical events, offering a unique perspective on these issues. This approach can be both enlightening and provocative, prompting readers to reevaluate their views.

Reflecting on the Human Condition Through Paradox

Paradoxes in memoirs can be a means of reflecting on the human condition. They allow memoirists to delve into the heart of human experiences, exploring how contradictory and complex emotions, beliefs, and behaviors are part of what makes us human.

The use of irony and paradox in memoirs adds richness and depth to the narrative. These literary devices allow memoirists to explore and convey the complexities of their experiences and observations in a nuanced and engaging way. By incorporating irony and paradox, memoirists can create a memoir that is not only a recounting of their life but also a profound exploration of the broader human experience, full of insights, reflections, and a deeper understanding of the paradoxical nature of life.

WRITING ABOUT LOVE AND RELATIONSHIPS

In memoir writing, delving into the intricacies of love and relationships is a profound and often central theme. These narratives provide a deep exploration of the memoirist's personal connections, offering insights into the joys, challenges, and complexities of love in its many forms. Whether it's romantic love, familial bonds, friendships, or even the relationship with oneself, these stories form an integral part of the memoir, reflecting the profound impact relationships have on the memoirist's life journey.

The Complexity of Romantic Relationships

Romantic relationships, with their highs and lows, often feature prominently in memoirs. Writing about romantic love involves exploring not just the joy and companionship these relationships bring but also the challenges, heartbreaks, and lessons learned. Memoirists might delve into how these relationships have shaped their understanding of love, trust, and partnership, often reflecting on personal growth that arises from these experiences.

Familial Bonds and Influences

Family relationships are another critical aspect of

many memoirs. These relationships can be complex, encompassing unconditional love, deep-seated conflicts, long-held resentments, and profound connections. Writing about family often involves navigating these multifaceted dynamics, exploring the impact of family on the memoirist's identity, values, and life choices. Memoirists might reflect on the influence of parents, the bonds with siblings, or the dynamics of extended family relations.

Friendships and Their Transformative Power

Friendships can play a transformative role in a person's life, and exploring these relationships in memoirs can offer a rich tapestry of shared experiences, support, and personal growth. Writing about friendships might involve recounting how these relationships have provided comfort, challenged the memoirist to grow, or offered a sense of belonging. It also might delve into the evolution of friendships over time, reflecting on how they have endured or changed as life circumstances shift.

Self-Discovery and Self-Love

An essential relationship that memoirists often explore is the relationship with themselves. This might involve a journey of self-discovery, self-acceptance, or self-love. Writing about this internal relationship can be introspective, involving an exploration of one's own character, aspirations, and inner conflicts. It often reflects the memoirist's journey towards understanding and accepting themselves, with all their flaws and strengths.

Navigating Loss and Grief

Love and relationships in memoirs often involve navigating

the terrain of loss and grief. Memoirists might recount the emotional journey of losing someone they love, whether through death, separation, or other circumstances. This exploration can be a powerful reflection on the nature of loss, the process of grieving, and ultimately, the resilience of the human spirit in the face of such experiences.

The Universal Resonance of Relationship Stories

Stories about love and relationships have a universal resonance, as they touch on experiences and emotions that are broadly relatable. By sharing their personal stories of love, memoirists can connect with readers on a deep level, evoking empathy, recognition, and emotional engagement.

The Impact of Cultural and Social Contexts

In discussing relationships, memoirists often consider the impact of cultural, social, and historical contexts. These contexts can shape how relationships are formed, experienced, and understood. For instance, cultural norms and societal expectations can influence romantic relationships, family dynamics, and even the way individuals perceive themselves.

Ethical Considerations in Writing About Others

When writing about relationships, memoirists face ethical considerations, especially regarding privacy and respect for the others involved in their stories. Balancing honesty and authenticity with sensitivity and respect is crucial. This might involve changing names or details to protect privacy or considering the potential impact of the memoir on the relationships and individuals featured.

Writing about love and relationships in memoirs offers a window into the most intimate and impactful aspects of the memoirist's life. These narratives, with their exploration of connections and emotions, form the heart of many memoirs. They provide readers with not only a glimpse into the memoirist's personal world but also a reflection on the universal experiences of love, loss, and the human desire for connection. Through these stories, memoirists can offer a rich, emotional, and nuanced exploration of the relationships that shape and define our lives.

PART XIV: RESPONSIBILITIES, ENDINGS AND EVOLUTION

The Memoirist's Responsibility to the Reader

In memoir writing, the memoirist holds a significant responsibility toward their readers. This responsibility extends beyond merely telling a story; it encompasses the ethical considerations of truthfulness, the impact of the memoir on its audience, and the broader implications of sharing a personal narrative. The memoirist's duty is to navigate these responsibilities thoughtfully, ensuring that their story is not only engaging and authentic but also respectful and considerate of the readers and the people featured in the narrative.

Truthfulness and Authenticity

The cornerstone of any memoir is its truthfulness and authenticity. Readers approach memoirs expecting a genuine account of the author's experiences and perceptions. The memoirist's responsibility is to honor this expectation by being as truthful and accurate as possible. This includes being honest about the limitations of memory and acknowledging any alterations or fictionalized elements in the narrative. Authenticity also involves presenting a multi-dimensional portrayal of events and people, including oneself, to avoid oversimplification or distortion.

Ethical Considerations in Storytelling

Memoirists also have ethical responsibilities in how they tell their story. This includes considering the privacy and dignity of people featured in the memoir, especially when dealing with sensitive or personal matters. The memoirist should balance their right to tell their story with the rights of others who are part of that story. This may involve anonymizing identities or changing details to protect privacy. Furthermore, the memoirist should be mindful of not causing harm or unnecessary distress through their narrative.

Navigating the Impact on Readers

Memoirists should be aware of the impact their story may have on readers. This includes considering how themes or content might affect people, especially if dealing with triggering or highly emotional subjects. Providing content warnings or thoughtful prefaces can prepare readers for challenging content. The memoirist's responsibility is to create a narrative that, while honest and unflinching, is also sensitive to the potential emotional responses of their audience.

Balancing Personal Expression with Public Perception

While a memoir is a deeply personal form of expression, it inevitably becomes a public artifact once published. The memoirist must navigate the balance between personal expression and public perception. This involves being aware of how the memoir contributes to broader conversations and societal narratives. The memoirist should be conscious of not perpetuating stereotypes or misinformation, especially when discussing issues like culture, identity, or social challenges.

The Role of Reflection and Insight

A memoirist's responsibility extends to providing reflection and insight, not just recounting events. Readers often seek memoirs for understanding, empathy, and connection. The memoirist should strive to offer thoughtful reflections and insights that emerge from their experiences, providing depth to the narrative and potentially offering readers new perspectives on similar experiences or feelings.

Fostering Understanding and Empathy

Memoirs have the power to foster understanding and empathy among readers. By sharing personal stories, memoirists can bridge gaps between different experiences and backgrounds. The responsibility here is to present a narrative that encourages empathy and understanding, allowing readers to see the world through someone else's eyes.

Representing a Larger Story

Often, a memoirist's personal story intersects with larger societal, historical, or cultural narratives. The memoirist has a responsibility to acknowledge and respect these larger contexts, understanding that their personal story is part of a bigger picture. This involves thoughtful consideration of how individual experiences reflect or contrast with broader societal issues or historical events.

Honoring the Memoir's Influence

Finally, memoirists should recognize and honor the influence their memoir may have. This includes understanding the memoir's potential role in shaping readers' perspectives, inspiring change, or offering comfort. With this influence comes the responsibility to use the memoir as a tool for positive impact, whether it's through inspiring others, advocating for change, or simply providing solace through shared experiences.

The responsibility of the memoirist to the reader is multi-faceted, encompassing ethical, emotional, and societal considerations. By navigating these responsibilities with care and thoughtfulness, memoirists can create narratives that are not only personal and authentic but also respectful, insightful, and impactful. The memoir then becomes more than just a story; it becomes a meaningful connection between the memoirist and their readers, and a valuable contribution to the tapestry of human experiences.

ADVANCED TECHNIQUES IN CRAFTING MEMOIR ENDINGS

Crafting the ending of a memoir is a significant aspect of the narrative process, requiring thoughtful consideration and skill. The ending is not merely a conclusion but a culmination of the memoirist's journey, a final note that resonates with the themes, experiences, and insights explored throughout the narrative. Advanced techniques in crafting memoir endings involve more than just bringing the story to a close; they aim to leave a lasting impact on the reader, providing closure, reflection, and often, a sense of continuity beyond the memoir's pages.

Resonating with the Memoir's Themes

A well-crafted ending resonates with the memoir's overarching themes. It should reflect the key ideas and insights that have been developed throughout the narrative, tying together the various threads of the story. Whether the memoir's themes revolve around personal growth, resilience, identity, or transformation, the ending should encapsulate these concepts, leaving the reader with a deeper understanding and appreciation of the memoirist's journey.

Providing Emotional Closure

The ending of a memoir should provide emotional closure for both the memoirist and the reader. This doesn't necessarily mean a resolution to all issues or challenges presented in the narrative but rather an acknowledgment of the journey undertaken and its emotional trajectory. The memoirist might reflect on how they have changed, what they have learned, or how they have come to terms with certain aspects of their story.

The Art of the Reflective Ending

Many memoirs employ a reflective ending, where the memoirist takes a moment to ponder the significance of their experiences. This reflection can be a powerful tool for connecting with readers, as it often delves into the universal aspects of the memoirist's story, inviting readers to contemplate their own lives and experiences in relation to the narrative.

Suggesting Continuity Beyond the Memoir

Memoirs, while encapsulating a specific portion of the memoirist's life, often suggest a sense of continuity beyond the scope of the narrative. The ending can hint at the ongoing nature of the memoirist's journey, acknowledging that life continues beyond the events of the memoir. This technique can leave readers with a sense of anticipation and curiosity about the memoirist's future.

The Use of Symbolism and Metaphor

Symbolism and metaphor can be effective in crafting a memoir's ending. By tying back to symbols or metaphors used throughout the memoir, the ending can achieve a sense of completeness and thematic unity. For example, a memoir that frequently references a particular journey might conclude with the memoirist reaching their destination, symbolizing the culmination of their personal journey.

Avoiding Neat Resolutions

While some memoirs might have neat, conclusive endings, many effective memoir endings avoid overly tidy resolutions, reflecting the complexity and ongoing nature of real life. Instead of wrapping up every storyline or answering every question, these endings acknowledge the messiness and open-endedness of life experiences.

The Power of the Last Line

The last line of a memoir holds significant weight. A powerful, well-crafted last line can leave a lasting impression on the reader, encapsulating the essence of the memoirist's story or offering a final insight. The memoirist might choose a line that echoes the opening of the memoir, comes full circle with an earlier theme, or leaves the reader with a poignant, thought-provoking statement.

Connecting with the Reader

Ultimately, the ending of a memoir should forge a connection with the reader. Whether through shared emotions, universal experiences, or insightful reflections, the ending should leave the reader feeling connected to the memoirist's story and perhaps, seeing aspects of their own life in a new light.

Crafting the ending of a memoir is a delicate balance of providing closure, resonating with the memoir's themes, and leaving a lasting impact on the reader. By employing advanced techniques, memoirists can create endings that are not only satisfying and reflective but also enriching, offering readers a sense of connection, understanding, and continuity that lingers long after the final page is turned.

BLURRING THE LINES BETWEEN FACT AND FICTION

In memoir writing, the intersection of fact and fiction is a complex and nuanced territory. While the core of a memoir is its adherence to truth and factual recounting of personal experiences, the narrative often navigates the blurry lines between reality and perception, memory and imagination. This interplay between fact and fiction in memoirs presents both challenges and opportunities for memoirists, allowing them to explore the fluid nature of memory and the creative aspects of recounting one's life story.

The Fluidity of Memory

Memory is inherently subjective and fluid. As memoirists recount their experiences, they often grapple with the elusive nature of memory. What is remembered and how it is remembered can be influenced by time, emotions, and subsequent experiences. This fluidity allows memoirists to explore their past from a current perspective, recognizing that memories might be colored or reshaped by their present understanding.

Creative Reconstruction of Events

Memoirists often engage in the creative reconstruction of events. While staying true to the facts, they might fill in gaps or recreate dialogues to the best of their ability. This process acknowledges that absolute accuracy in recalling past conversations or minor details is often impossible. The aim is to capture the essence and emotional truth of the experience, even if it requires some creative reconstruction.

The Narrative Arc in Memoirs

Crafting a compelling narrative arc sometimes involves structuring real-life events in ways that resemble fictional storytelling. This can mean selecting which events to include and how to pace them, creating a narrative that is engaging and coherent. The memoirist might employ storytelling techniques like foreshadowing, thematic development, and character arcs to enhance the narrative, bridging the gap between raw facts and a compelling story.

Honesty and Disclosure

Honesty and transparency are crucial in memoir writing, especially when navigating the line between fact and fiction. Memoirists often address the subjective nature of their narratives, acknowledging any creative liberties they have taken in the reconstruction of events. This disclosure helps maintain the integrity of the memoir, ensuring that the reader understands the balance between factual recounting and narrative craft.

The Role of Imagination

Imagination plays a subtle yet significant role in memoir

writing. It comes into play not in fabricating events but in imagining the emotions, motivations, and thoughts of the memoirist's past self or other characters in their story. This imaginative empathy allows memoirists to delve deeper into their experiences, offering a richer, more nuanced narrative.

Ethical Considerations

Navigating the interplay between fact and fiction in memoirs involves ethical considerations. Memoirists must be cautious not to mislead readers or misrepresent events or characters. The ethical responsibility involves balancing the creative aspects of memoir writing with a commitment to truthfulness and accuracy.

Reflecting on Perception and Reality

Memoirs often reflect on the themes of perception and reality. Memoirists might explore how their understanding of certain events has evolved over time or how different perspectives can yield different versions of the truth. This reflection can add a philosophical depth to the memoir, engaging readers in contemplating the nature of truth and memory.

The Impact on the Reader

The blending of fact and fiction in memoirs impacts how readers engage with the narrative. It invites readers to not only learn about the memoirist's life but also to ponder the nature of their own memories and perceptions. This engagement can make the memoir a more immersive and thought-provoking experience.

In memoir writing, blurring the lines between fact and fiction is an intricate dance. It requires a careful balance, a deep understanding of the nuances of memory, and a commitment to honesty. By navigating this territory skillfully, memoirists can create narratives that are not only faithful to their experiences but also rich in narrative depth and emotional resonance. This approach allows them to tell their stories in a way that is both authentic and artistically compelling, offering readers a window into the complex interplay of fact, memory, and narrative craft.

THE EVOLUTION OF THE MEMOIR GENRE

The memoir genre has experienced a significant transformation over the years, evolving from the documentation of prominent historical figures' lives to a platform for a diverse range of voices sharing personal, nuanced narratives. This evolution reflects broader societal, cultural, and technological changes, and has led to the memoir becoming a dynamic and multifaceted literary form.

Historical and Societal Influences

Originally, memoirs were often the domain of public figures recounting significant historical events and achievements. Over time, the genre expanded to include stories from individuals from various walks of life, providing insight into a broader spectrum of human experiences. This shift was influenced by societal changes, including movements for social justice and increased recognition of diverse perspectives. Contemporary memoirs frequently address themes like identity, mental health, and social issues, reflecting a societal shift towards greater inclusivity and openness.

Literary Developments in Memoir Writing

Literary trends have significantly shaped the memoir genre. The emergence of modernist and postmodernist literature, which emphasized subjective experience and non-linear narratives, broadened the scope and style of memoir writing. Today's memoirs often blend elements of fiction and non-fiction, pushing the boundaries of traditional narrative structures. The use of experimental formats, fragmented storytelling, and non-linear timelines is increasingly common, mirroring literary trends that favor innovation and creativity.

Impact of Technological Advances

Technological advancements have greatly influenced memoir writing and publication. The digital age, with its blogs, social media platforms, and self-publishing options, has democratized the memoir genre. More people have access to tools for writing and sharing their stories, leading to a proliferation of memoirs covering a wide range of experiences and perspectives. This technological revolution has not only increased the volume of memoirs available but has also diversified the voices represented in the genre.

Addressing Complex Themes

As cultural norms and societal conversations have evolved, memoirs have become a medium for exploring complex and previously taboo subjects. Discussions around mental health, gender identity, racial dynamics, and personal trauma are now more prevalent in memoirs. This openness reflects a cultural shift towards embracing and understanding diverse experiences and challenges, making memoirs a powerful tool for empathy and awareness.

The Role of Memory and Personal Interpretation

The subjective nature of memory plays a crucial role in memoir writing. Contemporary memoirists often grapple with the fallibility and fluidity of memory, acknowledging that personal narratives are shaped by individual perceptions and emotions. This focus on the interpretive nature of memory has led to a more introspective and exploratory form of memoir writing, where the emphasis is on understanding and conveying personal truths rather than objective facts.

Technological Integration and Future Trends

The integration of technology in storytelling is shaping the future trajectory of memoirs. With advancements in digital media, memoirists now have opportunities to incorporate multimedia elements, such as photographs, audio, and video, into their narratives. The future of memoirs may also see increased interactivity, where readers engage with the narrative in innovative ways, and the exploration of virtual and augmented reality as storytelling tools.

Ethical Considerations in Storytelling

The blurring of lines between fact and fiction in memoirs raises important ethical considerations. Memoirists navigate the challenge of portraying their experiences truthfully while respecting the privacy and perspectives of others featured in their stories. The ethical responsibility to balance personal expression with the potential impact on others featured in the narrative is a critical aspect of contemporary memoir writing.

The memoir genre's evolution is marked by a shift from historical chronicles to a form that embraces personal, subjective experiences, reflecting broader literary, societal, and technological changes. This evolution has made memoirs a more inclusive and versatile form of storytelling, offering insights into a wide array of human experiences and perspectives. As the genre continues to evolve, it promises to remain a vital and dynamic form of personal and collective expression.

THE MEMOIRIST AS A CULTURAL STORYTELLER

The role of a memoirist often transcends the mere recounting of personal experiences, elevating them to the status of cultural storytellers. In this capacity, memoirists not only share their individual stories but also reflect and comment on the broader cultural, social, and historical contexts in which they live. Their narratives become a lens through which readers can view and understand larger societal patterns, changes, and issues.

Reflecting Societal and Cultural Dynamics

Memoirists often find themselves at the intersection of personal experience and broader societal dynamics. By narrating their personal journeys, they inadvertently cast light on the cultural and social contexts that shape those experiences. This reflection can provide readers with insights into different cultures, social norms, and historical periods. Memoirists can offer a unique perspective on how larger societal forces such as politics, social movements, and cultural shifts impact individual lives.

Storytelling as a Means of Preservation

Memoirists play a crucial role in preserving cultural histories and narratives, especially those that might be marginalized or underrepresented. Through their stories, they keep alive the traditions, experiences, and voices of communities that might otherwise be overlooked. This act of preservation is particularly important in a rapidly changing world where cultural practices and histories risk being forgotten or overshadowed by dominant narratives.

Bridging Personal and Collective Experiences

One of the remarkable abilities of memoirists as cultural storytellers is to bridge the gap between personal and collective experiences. They narrate their individual stories in a way that resonates with broader audiences, allowing readers to see part of their own lives and experiences reflected in the memoir. This connection fosters a sense of shared humanity and can be particularly powerful in bringing to light common struggles, joys, and challenges.

Challenging Stereotypes and Broadening Perspectives

Through their narratives, memoirists have the opportunity to challenge stereotypes and broaden perspectives. By presenting complex and nuanced portrayals of their cultures, communities, and personal identities, they can counter simplistic or monolithic representations often seen in mainstream media. This role is crucial in promoting understanding and empathy across diverse cultural and social lines.

The Memoirist's Voice in Social Commentary

Memoirists often use their narratives as a platform for social commentary. They can highlight social injustices, cultural conflicts, and political issues through the lens of their personal experiences. This approach allows them to comment on and critique these issues in a way that is both informed by personal experience and relevant to broader societal conversations.

Reflecting on Change and Continuity

Memoirists can reflect on the themes of change and continuity within their cultural and social environments. They often witness and document significant societal changes, providing a personal perspective on how these changes manifest in everyday life. At the same time, they can also highlight the aspects of their culture and society that remain constant, offering a sense of continuity and connection to the past.

Contributing to Cultural Understanding and Dialogue

Memoirs contribute significantly to cultural understanding and dialogue. By sharing their stories, memoirists provide a medium for readers to engage with and learn about different cultures, experiences, and viewpoints. This contribution is invaluable in an increasingly interconnected world, where understanding and respecting cultural diversity is key to global harmony and cooperation.

Navigating Cultural Sensitivity and Authenticity

In their role as cultural storytellers, memoirists navigate the delicate balance between cultural sensitivity and authenticity. They must be mindful of how they represent their own and others' cultures, ensuring their narratives are respectful and do not perpetuate cultural misunderstandings or biases. At the same time, they strive to remain true to their experiences and perspectives, presenting an authentic and honest account of their lives.

As cultural storytellers, memoirists provide a vital link between the personal and the universal, offering narratives that are deeply individual yet resonate with larger cultural and societal themes. Through their memoirs, they contribute to the tapestry of human experience, enriching our understanding of the diverse world in which we live. Their stories serve not only as personal memoirs but as cultural artifacts, preserving and celebrating the richness of human life and society.

EMBRACING YOUR JOURNEY AS A MEMOIRIST

The journey of a memoirist is a profound and often transformative experience, encompassing not just the act of writing about one's life but also the introspective process of understanding and interpreting those experiences. This journey is unique for every memoirist, involving moments of self-discovery, challenges, and revelations. It is a journey that goes beyond simply documenting events; it involves delving into the depths of personal experience, extracting meaning, and sharing these insights in a way that resonates with others.

The Introspective Nature of Memoir Writing

Memoir writing is inherently introspective. It requires memoirists to look inward, revisiting and reflecting on significant moments of their lives. This introspection is not always easy, as it often involves confronting difficult, painful, or complex memories. However, it can also be a cathartic and enlightening process, offering memoirists a chance to understand their past, reconcile with it, and potentially find peace or closure.

The Evolution of Self-Understanding

As memoirists journey through their past, they often gain a deeper understanding of themselves. They might uncover motivations behind their actions, recognize patterns in their behavior, or see events in their life from a new perspective. This evolution of self-understanding is a crucial aspect of memoir writing, as it not only enriches the narrative but also contributes to personal growth and self-awareness.

Navigating the Challenges of Honesty and Vulnerability

Writing a memoir involves a delicate balance of honesty and vulnerability. Memoirists must be willing to expose their flaws, mistakes, and weaknesses, which can be both intimidating and liberating. The challenge lies in being authentically oneself while also being mindful of how the story might impact others involved. Striking this balance requires courage and integrity.

The Impact of Sharing Personal Stories

Sharing personal stories through a memoir can have a profound impact, both on the memoirist and the readers. For the memoirist, it can be a way to reclaim their narrative, heal from past experiences, or connect with others who have had similar experiences. For readers, a memoir can offer insights, inspiration, or a sense of solidarity, reminding them that they are not alone in their struggles or experiences.

The Role of Creativity and Expression

Memoir writing is not just a recounting of facts; it is a creative and expressive endeavor. Memoirists use literary techniques to craft a narrative that is compelling and evocative. This creative process is a significant part of the memoirist's journey, allowing them to transform raw experiences into a story that engages, moves, and impacts readers.

Learning and Growing Through Feedback

Receiving feedback is an integral part of the memoirist's journey. Constructive criticism from editors, peers, or readers can be invaluable, helping memoirists refine their narrative, deepen their insights, and improve their storytelling. This feedback can be challenging to receive but is essential for growth and development as a writer.

The Ongoing Journey Beyond Publication

The journey of a memoirist does not end with publication. Sharing their memoir with the world is just another phase of the journey, often leading to new connections, opportunities, and insights. The memoir becomes a living entity, continuously interacting with and impacting others, while the memoirist continues to grow and evolve from these interactions.

Embracing the Uniqueness of Each Memoirist's Path

Every memoirist's journey is unique, influenced by their personal experiences, writing style, and the particular challenges and revelations they encounter along the way. Embracing this uniqueness is crucial, as it is what makes each memoir distinct and authentic. The memoirist's journey is as much about the process of writing and self-exploration as it is about the final product.

The journey of a memoirist is a multifaceted and ongoing process, marked by introspection, creativity, and growth. It is a journey that transcends the pages of their memoir, influencing and being influenced by the wider world. For memoirists, embracing this journey with all its challenges and rewards is an integral part of sharing their life stories and connecting with a broader audience. Through their memoirs, they not only tell their stories but also contribute to the rich tapestry of human experience and understanding.

THE END

Printed in Great Britain
by Amazon